A
Call from
God

*Come to God through Jesus Christ and
into a blessed and eternal life.*

Come from the darkness into the light of life.

By

Elena N. Sifuentes

A Call from God
Copyright @ 2020 by Elena N. Sifuentes

All Rights Reserved. No portion of this book may be reproduced, stored in a retrieval system, or transmitted in any form or by any means - electronic, mechanical, photocopy, recording, scanning or other - except for brief quotations in critical reviews or articles, without the prior written permission of the publisher. Subject to permission under action 107 and/or 108 of the 1976 United States Copyright act. Request for permission should be addressed to the publisher web page.

First paperback edition October 2020

ISBN 978-1-7351400-2-5 (paperback)
ISBN 978-1-7351400-3-2 (eBook)

Published by Elena N. Sifuentes

Please note: Every effort has been made to ensure the accuracy of the information throughout this book. The information is believed to be accurate at the time of printing. The publisher and author are not responsible for errors or omissions for changes to details or the consequences of the reader's reliance on the information provided.

Readers are welcome to contact the publisher for comments, updates, or questions at elenasifuentes919@gmail.com.

Dedication

This book is dedicated to God the Father, Jesus Christ, our Savior, and the Holy Spirit, our helper. I am thankful for God's love, mercy, grace, and patience that He has bestowed upon His children.

To the readers, it is not by chance that you have picked this book but by the guidance of the Holy Spirit. God yearns for you to accept His Son so that He can bless you and have fellowship with you now and forever. Now is the time to accept Jesus Christ as your Savior and Lord.

Acknowledgment

Thankful for Catherine Olen, my niece, for her guidance, expertise, and patience. She is an entrepreneur, writer, and has published numerous books.

Ben L. Wells III (Son) for his continued encouragement throughout this process.

Donna Sifuentes, for her support and assistance.

Introduction

The call from God comes with compassion and heartfelt love for every one of us.

From the beginning, God created man to have fellowship with us while we are alive here on earth, our temporary home, and for eternity. Fellowship with God requires a two-way conversation. We speak to God when we seek his presence, through praying, singing, and worshiping Him. In turn, when we read the Bible, God speaks to us through His words. He will also speak to us through other Christians, our inner voice, in our quiet time, and one-on-one time with Him.

While thinking about how little I knew about God when I first became a Christian, I felt God was leading me to write this book as a guide to new believers and for those that do not have a grasp of what God requires of us.

Since the fall of man, many obstacles are thrown our way to create havoc in our lives. However, God wants us to seek Him for assistance to work through these obstacles. God will always work for our good. At times He may take us out of the situation, or He may carry us through it. But to receive the peace that only God can give, we need to accept His Son, Jesus Christ, as our personal Savior and Lord.

Now is the time to receive Jesus Christ as your Savior to enjoy all that He has for you.

Contents

Dedication iii

Acknowledgment v

Introduction..vii

Chapter 1 – Seek the Lord.. 1

Chapter 2 – God's Covenant 24
    Covenant of Works 25
    Covenant with Abraham, Isaac, and Jacob 28
    The Mosaic Covenant... 53
    The New Covenant... 56

Chapter 3 – God's Promise... 62
    God's Peace 62
    Peace Like a River 65
    Help in Times of Anxiety...................................... 68
    Help in Time of Temptation 71
    Jesus the Only Mediator to God the Father........... 74
    God Protects 78
    Care and Discipline for Our Good........................ 80
    God's Mercy and Grace.. 86
    God Calls Us to Repentance 91
    Eternal Salvation 97
    God Will Never Forsake Us 104

Chapter 4 – Free Will... 108

Chapter 5 – Instinct for God....................................... 126

Chapter 6 – How to Live Freely 141

Chapter 7 – Living a Christian Life 150
    Being Born Again 150
    Access to God 152
    Heart and Mind of Christ 155
    Love through Action 157
    Seek the Good in Others 159
    Supplication 161
    Show Humility 164
    Have a Servant's Attitude 166
    Confess Sins 169

Chapter 8 – Follow Jesus' Example 171
    Pray Without Ceasing 171
    Thank God 173
    Forgive 178
    Share the Gospel to Everyone 181
    Peacemaker 187

Chapter 9 – Now Is the Time 192

Chapter 10 – Conclusion 197

About the Authur 201

CHAPTER 1

Seek the Lord

The resounding voices of nature's howling echoed fear as I reminisced of days gone by. Trees swayed back and forth as if dancing the waltz, while from afar, lightning flashed across the sky, causing trees to bear the resemblance of monsters. Raindrops echoed the sounds of drums pounding on the pavement while thunder quaked sounds of whips snapping across the glowing skies, saying, "I am the Lord your God, listen to my call and come."

Strong forces of nature create havoc and instill a sense of terror. They create concern for one's life and property as these forces pass by until they eventually abate. When we are frightened by wild storms as seen across the world and in our backyard, have you ever wondered, "What is God doing or trying to tell us?" Tropical storms, earthquakes, floods, monsoons, hurricanes, and pandemics ring so loudly as if calling everyone to seek God, the creator of the universe. When calamity comes, people often turn to God for help, guidance, comfort, protection, and peace.

Calamity comes in various ways, as it was evident during the September 11, 2001, terrorist suicide attacks. According to Britannica, *suicide attack is* defined as:

> **Suicide bombing**, *an act in which an individual personally delivers explosives and detonates them to inflict the greatest possible damage, killing himself or herself in the process. Suicide bombings are particularly shocking on account of their indiscriminate nature, clearly intending to kill or injure anyone within range of the explosion, the victims being mostly unsuspecting civilians (though political figures and military personnel are frequently the main targets), and because of the evident willingness of the bombers to die by their own hands. Virtually all suicide bombings are linked to political causes or grievances. Unlike suicidal tactics born of desperation in war, such as Japan's kamikaze attacks during World War II, suicide bombing is deliberately employed by terrorists for calculated political effect. Indeed, because suicide bombers have the ability to move, avoid security measures, and choose their targets, they have been likened to a human "smart bomb" (or "poor man's smart bomb"). The damage inflicted by suicide bombings is both physical and psychological, and to inflict maximum damage, the bombers rely heavily on the element of surprise.*[1]

---

[1] https://www.britannica.com/topic/suicide-bombing

Islamic extremists, who are a part of the terrorist group Al-Qaeda, hijacked four airplanes and used them to attack the United States. The terrorist flew two of the planes into the twin towers of the World Trade Center in New York City. They flew another plane just outside of Washington D.C., hitting the Pentagon, the headquarters of the U. S. Department of Defense located in Arlington County, Virginia. The fourth plane crashed in a field in Somerset County, Pennsylvania. The devastation resulted in thousands of people killed or injured either by being trapped in buildings or while they were in flight. Some of the victims were first responders caught in the devastation while fighting the fires that raged and saving the lives of people trapped. Buildings were brought down and much more.

With such powerful events surrounding us, material items that wash away become a reminder that in a blink of an eye, everything can be swept away. Buildings and material things can be replaced, but the lives of our family and friends can easily become a memory as they depart from this temporary home called earth. However, there is good news. As a Christian, this life is not the final journey as we will meet again in heaven through eternal salvation in Jesus Christ.

There are numerous scriptures in the Bible to backup this information. Here are a couple of scriptures found in 1 Thessalonians 4:13-18 and John 14:1-3:

1. In 1 Thessalonians 4:13-18, Paul wrote to the believers who were mourning their lost

ones; he was comforting them when he told them that they would see each other again in heaven.

Brothers and sisters, we do not want you to be uninformed about those who sleep in death, so that you do not grieve like the rest of mankind, who have no hope. For we believe that Jesus died and rose again, and so we believe that God will bring with Jesus those who have fallen asleep in him. According to the Lord's word, we tell you that we who are still alive, who are left until the coming of the Lord, will certainly not precede those who have fallen asleep. For the Lord himself will come down from heaven, with a loud command, with the voice of the archangel and with the trumpet call of God, and the dead in Christ will rise first. After that, we who are still alive and are left will be caught up together with them in the clouds to meet the Lord in the air. And so we will be with the Lord forever.

1 Thessalonians 4:13-18
New International Version (NIV)

2. In John 14:1-3, while Jesus was forecasting His impending death and resurrection, He was comforting the disciples when He promised He would return for them.

> *"Do not let your hearts be troubled. You believe in God; believe also in me. My Father's house has many rooms; if that were not so, would I have told you that I am going there to prepare a place for you? And if I go and prepare a place for you, I will come back and take you to be with me that you also may be where I am. You know the way to the place where I am going."*
>
> *John 14:1-3*
> *New International Version (NIV)*

Seeking the Lord's presence requires a conscious commitment that is accomplished when we set our minds and heart on Him. The Hebrew word presence is often translated as "face." When we are reminded to seek after God, the scriptures are not implying that God is far or has stepped away, see Acts 17:27, but a reminder for us to consciously seek His presence. Seeking after God should be mimicked with the same dedication and persistence used to obtain wealth and fame. People will spend excessive hours at work to make the big bucks or practice over and over again, focusing on talents with the hope of becoming famous. In this same way, we should be seeking a personal relationship with God. He has already paid the price for us to obtain the gifts He has for us. The scriptures remind us to seek God first; see Matthew 6:33, with all your heart, soul, and mind. This is accomplished through prayer, meditation, and reading the Word of God as we magnify and worship Him as King of kings, Lord of lords, and Almighty God. In Isaiah 6:1-3 and Revelations 4:8, God is referred to as "Holy,

Holy, Holy Lord Almighty," an attribute which signifies that He is to be revered and praised with glory, honor, and majesty as the Most High God over all. There are times when we do not put our trust in God, or we are distracted by the many directions of life; family, work, church, and non-church activities. We consciously or unconsciously step away from God. Therefore, we are reminded to seek His face continuously with a mindful attitude.

> *God did this so that they would seek him and perhaps reach out for him and find him, though he is not far from any one of us.*
> *Acts 17:27*
> *New International Version (NIV)*

> *But seek first His kingdom and His righteousness, and all these things will be added to you.*
> *Matthew 6:33*
> *King James Version (KJV)*

> *In the year that King Uzziah died, I saw the Lord, high and exalted, seated on a throne; and the train of his robe filled the temple. Above him were seraphim, each with six wings: With two wings they covered their faces, with two they covered their feet, and with two they were flying. And they were calling to one another: "Holy, holy, holy is the*

Lord Almighty; the whole earth is full of his glory."

Isaiah 6:1-3
New International Version (NIV)

"'Holy, holy, holy is the Lord God Almighty,' who was, and is, and is to come."

Revelations 4:8
New International Version (NIV)

Loving God, Jesus Christ, the Holy Spirit, and the love for humankind are the most valuable assets we have, and this should be cherished and embraced. In Romans 8:35-39, Apostle Paul declared that no one could separate us from the love of God, even through hard times. John 10:28 also states that no one will snatch His children from His hand. God loves every one of us, and His love is everlasting, as stated in Psalm 136:26, Psalm 103:17, and Jeremiah 31:3.

> *Who shall separate us from the love of Christ? Shall trouble or hardship or persecution or famine or nakedness or danger or sword? As it is written:*
>
> *"For your sake we face death all day long; we are considered as sheep to be slaughtered." No, in all these things we are more than conquerors through him who loved us. For I am convinced that neither death nor life, neither angels nor demons, neither the present nor the future, nor any powers, neither height nor depth, nor anything else in all creation,*

will be able to separate us from the love of God that is in Christ Jesus our Lord.

Romans 8:35-39
English Standard Version (ESV)

I give them eternal life, and they shall never perish; no one will snatch them out of my hand.

John 10:28
New International Version (NIV)

Give thanks to the God of heaven. His love endures forever.

Psalm 136:26
New International Version (NIV)

But from everlasting to everlasting the Lord's love is with those who fear him, and his righteousness with their children's children —
Psalm 103:17
New International Version (NIV)

The Lord appeared to us in the past, saying: "I have loved you with an everlasting love.
Jeremiah 31:3
New International Version (NIV)

Jesus commands everyone to love the Lord with all their heart, soul, mind, and strength and love one another. We show love for our neighbors when we witness to them verbally, or for example, through living an exemplary life to encourage others to want the peace they see in us. By your righteous influence, a curiosity for the gospel of Jesus Christ will begin to develop. Witnessing others will reinforce our desire to keep in line with God's will; that is, He does not want anyone to perish; see 2 Peter 3:9. The following verses command us to love God and our neighbor; see Luke 10:27, Mark 12:29-31, Matthew 22:36-40, and Deuteronomy 10:12.

> *The Lord is not slow in keeping his promise, as some understand slowness. Instead he is patient with you, not wanting anyone to perish, but everyone to come to repentance.*
> *2 Peter 3:9*
> *New International Version (NIV)*

> *He answered, "'Love the Lord your God with all your heart and with all your soul and with all your strength and with all your mind'; and, 'Love your neighbor as yourself.'"*
> *Luke 10:27*
> *New International Version (NIV)*

> *"The most important one," answered Jesus, "is this: 'Hear, O Israel: The Lord our God, the Lord is one. Love the Lord your God with all your heart and with all your soul and with all your mind and with all your strength.' The second is this: 'Love your neighbor as yourself.' There is no commandment greater than these."*
> *Mark 12:29-31*
> *New International Version (NIV)*

> *"Teacher, which is the greatest commandment in the Law?"*
>
> *Jesus replied: "'Love the Lord your God with all your heart and with all your soul and with all your mind.' This is the first and greatest commandment. And the second is like it: 'Love your neighbor as yourself.' All the Law and the Prophets hang on these two commandments."*
>
> *Matthew 22:36-40*
> *New International Version (NIV)*

> *And now, Israel, what does the Lord your God ask of you but to fear the Lord your God, to walk in obedience to him, to love him, to serve the Lord your God with all your heart and with all your soul, and to observe the Lord's commands and decrees that I am giving you today for your own good?*
>
> *Deuteronomy 10:12*
> *New International Version (NIV)*

In 1 Chronicles 16:1, we are instructed to not only seek His face but His strength. Our strength comes from the Lord when we read the word, pray, and praise Him. Isaiah 40:31 reminds us that when we put our trust in the Lord, and when we grow weary, He will renew our strength.

> *Look to the Lord and his strength; seek his face always.*
>
> *1 Chronicles 16:11*
> *New International Version (NIV)*

> *Even youths grow tired and weary, and young men stumble and fall; but those who hope in the Lord will renew their strength. They will soar on wings like eagles; they will run and not grow weary; they will walk and not be faint.*
> *Isaiah 40:30-31*
> *New International Version (NIV)*

While listening to "*You Raise Me Up*" sung by Josh Groban, I was encouraged by the words, "You raise me up to be more than I can be." I believe this is what God wants to do for His children. God wants to strengthen His children so they will accomplish more than what they can ask or imagine; see Ephesians 3:20.

> *Now to him who is able to do immeasurably more than all we ask or imagine, according to his power that is at work within us.*
> *Ephesians 3:20*
> *New International Version (NIV)*

We are not to neglect the assembly or fellowship with other Christians so that we can encourage and comfort one another, see Hebrew 10:24-25.

> *And let us consider how we may spur one another on toward love and good deeds, not giving up meeting together, as some are in the habit of doing, but encouraging one another —and all the more as you see the Day approaching.*
> *Hebrew 10:24-25*
> *New International Version (NIV)*

An example I heard many years ago and still like to use is the illustration of the coals in a fire pit:

> "If you take one coal out of the fire and set it aside, without fuel, it will die, but if you keep feeding the fire with coals, it will continue to be strengthened as it continues to burn."

Similarly, our thoughts of God can diminish over time when we neglect and do not seek God mindfully.

Here is an example of why we should not neglect to go to church or keep in fellowship with other believers:

> In my younger days and before I understood what it meant to be a Christian, I knew I should go to church every Sunday, but one of my close friends said, "You know you don't have to go to church every Sunday." So, I began to think, "I went to church last Sunday, so I will skip this Sunday." Before I knew it, I had stopped going to church. But when my life was changed by unwanted obstacles and found myself in need of God, I began to seek Him for help, guidance, and comfort.

The following verses remind us to always devote our hearts and soul to seeking the Lord, seek His face, and to seek His strength; 1 Chronicles 22:19, Psalm 105:4, Colossians 3:1-

2, Isaiah 55:6-7, 1Chronicles 16:11, Nehemiah 8:10, and Isaiah 41:10.

> *Now devote your heart and soul to seeking the Lord your God.*
>
> *1Chronicles 22:19*
> *New International Version (NIV)*

> *Look to the Lord and his strength; seek his face always.*
>
> *Psalm 105:4*
> *New International Version (NIV)*

> *Since, then, you have been raised with Christ, set your hearts on things above, where Christ is, seated at the right hand of God. Set your minds on things above, not on earthly things.*
>
> *Colossians 3:1-2*
> *New International Version (NIV)*

> *Seek the Lord while he may be found; call upon him while he is near; let the wicked forsake his way, and the unrighteous man his thoughts; let him return to the Lord, that he may have compassion on him, and to our God, for he will abundantly pardon.*
>
> *Isaiah 55:6-7*
> *English Standard Version (ESV)*

Seek the Lord and his strength, seek his face continually.

> *1 Chronicles 16:11*
> *King James Version*
> *King James Version (KJV).*

Do not grieve, for the joy of the Lord is your strength.

> *Nehemiah 8:10*
> *New International Version (NIV)*

So do not fear, for I am with you; do not be dismayed, for I am your God. I will strengthen you and help you; I will uphold you with my righteous right hand.

> *Isaiah 41:10*
> *New International Version (NIV)*

First, seek the Lord and trust Him. This should be our primary goal of living a Christian life. In Matthew 6:33, the Bible instructs us to seek the Lord and His righteousness with a promise that all things will be added to you so that in times of trouble and temptation, we will be equipped and strengthen through daily prayer and reading the word to stand firm. In an article written by Robert McFarland, he revealed statistical differences from those that read the Bible regularly from the infrequent reader.

> "A lack of scriptural engagement produces several consequences. Disengagement from God's word has left American believers ignorant of basic Bible facts and

> truths, vulnerable to false teachings, and, in many cases, spiritually immature. As our research has demonstrated, those who read the Bible at least four times a week are less likely to engage in behaviors such as gambling, pornography, getting drunk, and sex outside marriage. …
>
> In sum, these analyses confirm what CBE's initial research with Christ-followers revealed: there is a powerful relationship between engaging scripture at least four times a week and moral behavior. Among adults, reading or listening to the Bible at least four times a week lowers the odds of engaging in harmful behaviors such as getting drunk, having sex outside marriage, watching pornography, and gambling. These effects remain even after we have control for other factors, such as church attendance. Perhaps more important is the fact that we find no statistically significant differences between those who read or listen to the Bible only one to three days a week and those who do not at all."[2]

Additionally, for centuries, people have questioned the validity of the Bible. In the following articles, the accuracy of the Bible is proven, and thus, another reason to read the Word of God with confidence daily. In the article

---

[2] https://www.robertmcfarland.net/the-power-of-4/

"Clarifying Christianity," the author explains that there are scientific findings that validate the truth in the Bible. In "The Second Law of Thermodynamics," science has provided the validity of Psalm 102:25-26, which states earth and the heavens will all wear out like a garment. In "Score One for the Bible," archaeologists have evidence that the Jericho Wall had suddenly fallen as stated in the scriptures and the dates matched.

1. "Science and the Bible - Clarifying Christianity": The purpose of this page is not to explain what a great science text the Bible is, but to show that it is consistent with scientific facts. Still, the Bible mentions some things that we cannot explain. If God is really God, He should have the ability to do some things we cannot explain. In the last 100 years (especially in the last ten), scientists discovered many proofs that confirm the Bible's accuracy. Since these proofs support the accuracy of the text we can understand scientifically, it makes sense to trust the Bible's text we cannot yet understand.[3]

2. In Psalm 102: 25-26, the scripture reveals that earth and the heavens will wear out like a garment. In the article written by Duane Gish, PH.D. "The Second Law of Thermodynamics" confirms Psalm 102:26.

---

[3] http://www.clarifyingchristianity.com/science.shtml

"According to this Scripture, written three thousand years before the dawn of modern science, we learn that the universe is like a suit of clothes that is wearing out. In other words, the universe is running down, deteriorating, constantly becoming less and less orderly. The fact that the universe, in its present state is deteriorating, has been fully verified by modern science. Everywhere we look, from the scale of the galaxies down to the scale of the atom, we find a universal, natural tendency of all systems to go from order to disorder, from complexity to simplicity. Thus, clusters of galaxies are dispersing as the galaxies move away from one another. This natural tendency towards disorder is so all-pervasive and unfailing that it has been formalized as natural law - the Second Law of Thermodynamics. Isaac Asimov has stated it this way (Smithsonian Institute Journal, June 1970, p.6): "Another way of stating the second law then is: 'The universe is constantly getting more disorderly!' Viewed that way, we can see the Second Law is all about us. All we have to do is nothing, and everything deteriorates, collapses, breaks down, wears out - all by itself - and that is what the Second Law is all about." There is certainly no doubt, then, that modern scientific research has verified the truths expressed in Psalm 102:26. Many years of careful measurements by scientists, repeated many thousands of times, established beyond doubt the scientific truths expressed in that verse of Scripture."[4]

In the beginning you laid the foundations of the earth, and the heavens are the work of your hands. They will perish, but you remain;
Psalm 102:2- 26
New International Version (NIV)

3. The March 5, 1990 issue of Time magazine featured an article called,

"Score One for the Bible." In it, archaeologist Kathleen Kenyon claimed Jericho's walls had fallen suddenly. Many scholars feel this was caused by an earthquake, which may also explain the damming of the Jordan. Additionally, grain was discovered, which shows the city was conquered quickly. These findings add

---

[4] https://www.icr.org/article/modern-scientific-discoveries-verify-scriptures/--------

credence to the biblical account. Further study by Brian Wood found the date of the fall of Jericho to match the Bible's date.[5]

> *When the trumpets sounded, the army shouted, and at the sound of the trumpet, when the men gave a loud shout, the wall collapsed; so, everyone charged straight in, and they took the city.*
>
> *Joshua 6:20*
> *New International Version (NIV)*

God's righteousness is the only way to live what is pleasing to God; that is, we abstain from sinful desires which wage war against the soul; see 1 Peter 2:11-12.

> *But seek first the kingdom of God and his righteousness, and all these things will be added to you.*
>
> *Matthew 6:33*
> *English Standard Version (ESV)*

> *Dear friends, I urge you, as foreigners and exiles, to abstain from sinful desires, which wage war against your soul. Live such good lives among the pagans that, though they accuse you of doing wrong, they may see your*

---

[5] https://www.cru.org/us/en/train-and-grow/spiritual-growth/the-authority-of-scripture.html

> *good deeds and glorify God on the day he visits us.*
>
> 1 Peter 2:11-12
> New International Version (NIV)

When seeking the Lord, He opens the doors to an abundant life filled with His promises to live a fulfilled life embraced with His peace. He will carry his children through trial and tribulation with an everlasting peace that surpasses all understanding that the world can never comprehend. When the world says we should be upset, frustrated, aggravated, or take revenge, we will experience peace from God when we do not succumb to the temptations of worldly views and are obedient by following the teachings recorded in the Bible.

Worldly teachings can oppose Godly teachings when ungodly men make laws. The difference between Legal Law and Moral Law, as defined by The Free Dictionary and Merriam Webster Dictionary, is as follow:

> *Legal Law: A body of rules of conduct of binding legal force and effect, prescribed, recognized, and enforced by controlling authority*[6].
>
> *Moral Law: A general rule of right living especially: such a rule or group of rules conceived as universal and unchanging and as having the sanction of God's will,*

---

[6] https://legal-dictionary.thefreedictionary.com/law

> *of conscience, of man's moral nature, or of natural justice as revealed to human reason the basic protection of rights is the moral law based on man's dignity[7].*

Often laws are passed that go against the word of God, but just because the world says it is permissible, we must still follow the teachings recorded in the Bible. Abortion had become a sad turn of events since 1973 when the U. S. Supreme Court ruled in favor of Roe vs. Wade, allowing a woman to choose to have an abortion without excessive government limitations. This is murder, and we are commanded in Exodus 20:13 not to murder. Just because someone does not want the responsibility to raise a child or state, they are not ready to be a mother is not an excuse to abort the child, nor is it allowed scripturally. Even if a woman is raped, we are not to abort the baby because the parent will be punished for his sins; see Deuteronomy 24:26. However, there are other ways to handle this; if it is too painful to raise the child, consider placing the baby in the hands of caring people who can love and adopt the baby as many people are waiting to adopt. Children are a gift and a blessing from God; therefore, we should cherish, love, and care for them. See Psalm 127:3 and Psalm 139:13-16.

> *You shall not murder.*
>
> *Exodus 20:13*
> *New International Version (NIV)*

---

[7] https://www.merriam-webster.com/dictionary/moral%20law

Parents are not to be put to death for their children, nor children put to death for their parents; each will die for their own sin.
Deuteronomy 24:16
New International Version (NIV)

Behold, children are a gift of the Lord, The fruit of the womb is a reward.
Psalm 127:3
New American Standard Bible (NASB)

This is what the Lord says—your Redeemer, who formed you in the womb.
Isaiah 44:24
New International Version (NIV)

For you created my inmost being; you knit me together in my mother's womb.

I praise you because I am fearfully and wonderfully made; your works are wonderful, I know that full well. My frame was not hidden from you when I was made in the secret place, when I was woven together in the depths of the earth.

Your eyes saw my unformed body; all the days ordained for me were written in your book before one of them came to be.
Psalm 139:13-16
New International Version (NIV)

We are to seek the Lord and be careful not to allow our hearts to harden with worldly distractions because then we are choosing a life leading to destruction while in this earthly home and through eternity.

CHAPTER 2

God's Covenant

There are several covenants recorded in the Bible, but in this book, I am going to discuss four of the covenants God made: The Covenant of Works made with Adam and Eve; The Covenant made with Abraham, Isaac, and Jacob; The Mosaic Covenant; and the New Covenant.

A covenant is an agreement between two parties. The definition, according to the New Oxford Dictionary about the *Law* and *Theology of a covenant is as follows*:

> *Law: A formal agreement, contract, or promise in writing, especially one undertaking to make regular payments to a charity.*
>
> *1.1 Law - A clause in a contract drawn up by deed.*
>
> *1.2 Theology - An agreement which brings about a relationship of commitment between God and his people. The Jewish faith is*

> *based on the biblical covenants made with Abraham, Moses, and David.*[8]

- Covenant of Works

The recording of God's covenant made with Adam and Eve begins in the books of Genesis 1 and 2; it is known as the covenant of works, the covenant of creation, or covenant of life.

God had promised Adam an abundant and eternal life if he would be obedient and comply with the terms God had given him. All that was required of Adam was to watch and care over the garden, be fruitful, multiply in numbers, and he was to rule over the earth, including all livings creatures and plants. This covenant would have secured a harmonious life and eternal salvation, not only for Adam but for all of his descendants. The covenant provided everything Adam and Eve would need with only one condition; to not eat from the tree of knowledge of good and evil. This information is found in these two passages recorded in Genesis 1:28-31 and Genesis 2:15-17.

> *God blessed them and said to them, "Be fruitful and increase in number; fill the earth and subdue it. Rule over the fish in the sea and the birds in the sky and over every living creature that moves on the ground."*
>
> *Then God said, "I give you every seed-bearing plant on the face of the whole earth*

---

[8] https://en.oxforddictionaries.com/definition/covenant

and every tree that has fruit with seed in it. They will be yours for food. And to all the beasts of the earth and all the birds in the sky and all the creatures that move along the ground—everything that has the breath of life in it—I give every green plant for food." And it was so. God saw all that he had made, and it was very good.

Genesis 1:28-31
New International Version (NIV)

The Lord God took the man and put him in the Garden of Eden to work it and take care of it. And the Lord God commanded the man, "You are free to eat from any tree in the garden; but you must not eat from the tree of the knowledge of good and evil, for when you eat from it you will certainly die."

Genesis 2:15-17
New International Version (NIV)

However, Eve was deceived by the crafty serpent to eat from the forbidden tree, and so she and Adam ate from it. She saw that the forbidden fruit was good for food, pleasing to the eye, and for gaining wisdom; instead, this proved to be the fall of man, also called "The Fall." Before the fall, they walked in innocent obedience in the presence of God, but when they sinned, God cast them out of His presence. Therefore, their eyes were opened, and they were no longer innocent to their nakedness, as stated in Genesis 3:7.

> *Then the eyes of both of them were opened, and they realized they were naked; so they sewed fig leaves together and made coverings for themselves.*
>
> *Genesis 3:7*
> *New International Version (NIV)*

There were consequences for being disobedient; instead of just watching over the garden and enjoying the blessings of God's creation, God necessitates Adam to work hard to get food. Adam would have to plow and take care of the ground to harvest it. God cursed the ground, and thus it produced thorns and thistles which painfully became a reminder of their disobedience. Eve's punishment, in turn, would require severely painful childbearing experiences as a result of rejecting God's sovereignty. Genesis 3:17-19 and Genesis 3:16a describes the consequences:

> *To Adam he said, "Because you listened to your wife and ate fruit from the tree about which I commanded you, 'You must not eat from it,' "Cursed is the ground because of you; through painful toil you will eat food from it all the days of your life. It will produce thorns and thistles for you, and you will eat the plants of the field. By the sweat of your brow you will eat your food until you return to the ground, since from it you were taken; for dust you are and to dust you will return."*
>
> *Genesis 3:17-19*
> *New International Version (NIV)*

> *To the woman he said, "I will make your pains in childbearing very severe; with painful labor you will give birth to children.*
> *Genesis 3:16a*
> *New International Version (NIV)*

Disobedience does not have to be the final step taken in this life. God forgives everyone that humbly repents and accepts Jesus as their Savior and Lord. Just as we can repent, so was Adam and Eve; however, the scripture does not reveal whether they ever did. Therefore, we are instructed to accept Jesus and to repent today. Time flies by, and the longer we ignore the call to come to God, the greater the chances of not repenting, especially if we allow our hearts to be hardened towards God. Make the decision to repent today and become a child of God through Jesus Christ, and you will become a member of the family of God, an heir of God our Heavenly Father, and co-heir with Jesus Christ.

- Covenant with Abraham, Isaac, and Jacob

In this covenant, God first made the promise to Abraham, which was sworn by an oath to his son Isaac and then confirmed to Jacob, Abraham's grandson as a decree, see Psalm 105:8-10. This covenant was made with God's chosen people, the Israelites, the Jews who would produce the Messiah, Jesus Christ, the Savior. Deuteronomy 7:6-8 refers to God's chosen people as the Israelites, who were redeemed from the hands of Pharaoh. God promised to take care of them and their many descendants, save them and give them the Promised Land. In Genesis 50:24, when Joseph was nearing the end of his life, he encouraged his brothers by telling them that God would take them to the Promised Land. This area is described in Exodus 23:31 as the territory from the River of Egypt (the Red Sea) to the Mediterranean Sea and from the desert to the Euphrates River. In Numbers 34:1-12, the territory is described as a spacious land flowing with milk and honey; see Exodus 3:8.

> *He remembers his covenant forever, the promise he made, for a thousand generations, the covenant he made with Abraham, the oath he swore to Isaac.*
>
> *He confirmed it to Jacob as a decree, to Israel as an everlasting covenant.*
>
> *Psalm 105:8-10*
> *New International Version (NIV)*

> *For you are a people holy to the Lord your God. The Lord your God has chosen you to be a people for his treasured possession, out of all the peoples who are on the face of the earth. It was not because you were more in number than any other people that the Lord set his love on you and chose you, for you were the fewest of all peoples, but it is because the Lord loves you and is keeping the oath that he swore to your fathers, that the Lord has brought you out with a mighty hand and*

redeemed you from the house of slavery, from the hand of Pharaoh king of Egypt.

Deuteronomy 7:6-8
English Standard Version (ESV)

And Joseph said to his brothers, "I am about to die, but God will visit you and bring you up out of this land to the land that he swore to Abraham, to Isaac, and to Jacob."

Genesis 50:24
English Standard Version (ESV)

"I will establish your borders from the Red Sea to the Mediterranean Sea, and from the desert to the Euphrates River.

Exodus 23-31
New International Version (NIV)

The Lord said to Moses, "Command the Israelites and say to them: 'When you enter Canaan, the land that will be allotted to you as an inheritance is to have these boundaries:
"'Your southern side will include some of the Desert of Zin along the border of Edom. Your southern boundary will start in the east from the southern end of the Dead Sea, cross south of Scorpion Pass, continue on to Zin and go south of Kadesh Barnea. Then it will go to Hazar Addar and over to Azmon, where it

will turn, join the Wadi of Egypt and end at the Mediterranean Sea.
Numbers 34:1-12
New International Version (NIV)

So I have come down to rescue them from the hand of the Egyptians and to bring them up out of that land into a good and spacious land, a land flowing with milk and honey.
Exodus 3:8
New International Version (NIV)

This covenant starts with obedience to God's commandments, the Law also known as the Law of Moses and Prophets. These laws are written in the first five books of the Old Testament called the Torah, as referred to in Hebrew and the Pentateuch in Greek. Christian and Jewish tradition arranges the Prophets in different groups. The first group consists of Joshua, Judges, I and II Samuel, and I and II Kings; the second group consists of Isaiah, Jeremiah, and Ezekiel; and the third group is Hosea, Joel Amos, Obadiah, Jonah, Micah, Nahum, Habakkuk, Zephaniah, Haggai, Zechariah, and Malachi.

God would provide for their daily needs; they would be prosperous and blessed, He would give them peace and protect them. In Leviticus 26:3-13, the scriptures point out what would happen when they followed the decrees by being obedient to God.

"'If you follow my decrees and are careful to obey my commands, I will send you rain in

its season, and the ground will yield its crops and the trees their fruit. Your threshing will continue until grape harvest and the grape harvest will continue until planting, and you will eat all the food you want and live in safety in your land. "'I will grant peace in the land, and you will lie down and no one will make you afraid. I will remove wild beasts from the land, and the sword will not pass through your country. You will pursue your enemies, and they will fall by the sword before you. Five of you will chase a hundred, and a hundred of you will chase ten thousand, and your enemies will fall by the sword before you. "'I will look on you with favor and make you fruitful and increase your numbers, and I will keep my covenant with you. You will still be eating last year's harvest when you will have to move it out to make room for the new. I will put my dwelling place among you, and I will not abhor you. I will walk among you and be your God, and you will be my people. I am the Lord your God, who brought you out of Egypt so that you would no longer be slaves to the Egyptians; I broke the bars of your yoke and enabled you to walk with heads held high.

Leviticus 26:3-13
New International Version (NIV)

In Deuteronomy 28:1-2, God's covenant emphasizes the requirement to be fully obedient to receive His blessings:

> *If you fully obey the Lord your God and carefully follow all his commands I give you today, the Lord your God will set you high above all the nations on earth. All these blessings will come on you and accompany you if you obey the Lord your God.*
>
> *Deuteronomy 28:1-2*
> *New International Version (NIV)*

If we seek the Lord and love Him, He promises long and eternal life as seen in Psalm 91:14-16 and Proverbs 9:1. This occurs when we deny our will to follow and be obedient to His will. He will grant blessings and protection, and He will open the storehouse of His bounty. He rewards those that follow Him. He will answer when called upon, and He promises joy and peace. Also, because of His love, He will show Himself to us, as seen in John 14:21.

> *"Because he loves me," says the Lord, "I will rescue him; I will protect him, for he acknowledges my name. He will call on me, and I will answer him; I will be with him in trouble, I will deliver him and honor him. With long life I will satisfy him and show him my salvation."*
>
> *Psalm 91:14-16*
> *New International Version (NIV)*

> *For through wisdom your days will be many,*
> *and years will be added to your life.*
> > *Proverbs 9:11*
> > *New International Version (NIV)*

> *Whoever has my commands and keeps them is*
> *the one who loves me. The one who loves me*
> *will be loved by my Father, and I too will love*
> *them and show myself to them."*
> > *John 14:21*
> > *New International Version (NIV)*

Abraham– God's covenant with Abraham is found in Genesis 17:1-27 called the *Covenant of Circumcision*. The covenant was a requirement for Abraham and every male in his household to be circumcised; this included future generations. Abraham is a Hebrew name, which means "father of multitudes." Abraham was 99 years old when God appeared to him and made the covenant that if Abraham would walk in faithfulness and be blameless, He would increase his family and be the father of many nations. During this time, God had changed Abraham's name from Abram and promised to be his God, and this promise included his descendants to all generations as an everlasting covenant. Abraham resided in Canaan as a foreigner, and God gave him that land as an everlasting possession. Also, God promised to bless all that blessed him and curse all that cursed him. Here is the scripture:

> *When Abram was ninety-nine years old, the*
> *Lord appeared to him and said, "I am God*
> *Almighty; walk before me faithfully and be*

blameless. Then I will make my covenant between me and you and will greatly increase your numbers."

Abram fell facedown, and God said to him, "As for me, this is my covenant with you: You will be the father of many nations. No longer will you be called Abram; your name will be Abraham, for I have made you a father of many nations. I will make you very fruitful; I will make nations of you, and kings will come from you. I will establish my covenant as an everlasting covenant between me and you and your descendants after you for the generations to come, to be your God and the God of your descendants after you. The whole land of Canaan, where you now reside as a foreigner, I will give as an everlasting possession to you and your descendants after you; and I will be their God."

Then God said to Abraham, "As for you, you must keep my covenant, you and your descendants after you for the generations to come. This is my covenant with you and your descendants after you, the covenant you are to keep: Every male among you shall be circumcised. You are to undergo circumcision, and it will be the sign of the covenant between me and you. For the generations to come every male among you who is eight days old must be circumcised, including those born in your household or bought with money from a foreigner—those who are not your offspring. Whether born in your household or bought with your money, they must be circumcised. My covenant in your flesh is to be an everlasting covenant. Any uncircumcised male, who has not been circumcised in the flesh, will be cut off from his people; he has broken my covenant."

God also said to Abraham, "As for Sarai your wife, you are no longer to call her Sarai; her name will be Sarah. I will bless her and will surely give you a son by her. I will bless her so that she will be the mother of nations; kings of peoples will come from her."

Abraham fell facedown; he laughed and said to himself, "Will a son be born to a man a hundred years old? Will Sarah bear a child at the age of ninety?" And Abraham said to God, "If only Ishmael might live under your blessing!"

Then God said, "Yes, but your wife Sarah will bear you a son, and you will call him Isaac. I will establish my covenant with him as an everlasting covenant for his descendants after him. And as for Ishmael, I have heard you: I will surely bless him; I will make him fruitful and will greatly increase his numbers. He will be the father of twelve rulers, and I will make him into a great nation. But my covenant I will establish with Isaac, whom Sarah will bear to you by this time next year." When he had finished speaking with Abraham, God went up from him.

On that very day Abraham took his son Ishmael and all those born in his household or bought with his money, every male in his household, and circumcised them, as God told him. Abraham was ninety-nine years old when he was circumcised, and his son Ishmael was thirteen; Abraham and his son Ishmael were both circumcised on that very day. And every male in Abraham's household, including those born in his household or bought from a foreigner, was circumcised with him.

Genesis 17:1-27
English Standard Version (ESV)

Isaac - As God promised, He gave Abraham a son through Sarah, and God established a covenant with his son, Isaac. The covenant God made with Isaac was the result of Abraham's obedience and faithfulness to God. God promised Isaac an innumerable seed, the Promised Land (the whole land of Canaan), and through his seed, all nations would be blessed. This covenant also included the lineage that produced Jesus Christ. The lineage is found in Matthew 1:1-17:

> *This is the genealogy of Jesus the Messiah the son of David, the son of Abraham: Abraham was the father of Isaac, Isaac the father of Jacob, Jacob the father of Judah and*

his brothers, Judah the father of Perez and Zerah, whose mother was Tamar, Perez the father of Hezron, Hezron the father of Ram, Ram the father of Amminadab, Amminadab the father of Nahshon, Nahshon the father of Salmon, Salmon the father of Boaz, whose mother was Rahab, Boaz the father of Obed, whose mother was Ruth, Obed the father of Jesse, and Jesse the father of King David. David was the father of Solomon, whose mother had been Uriah's wife, Solomon the father of Rehoboam, Rehoboam the father of Abijah, Abijah the father of Asa, Asa the father of Jehoshaphat, Jehoshaphat the father of Jehoram, Jehoram the father of Uzziah, Uzziah the father of Jotham,

Jotham the father of Ahaz, Ahaz the father of Hezekiah, Hezekiah the father of Manasseh, Manasseh the father of Amon, Amon the father of Josiah, and Josiah the father of Jeconiah and his brothers at the time of the exile to Babylon. After the exile to Babylon:

Jeconiah was the father of Shealtiel, Shealtiel the father of Zerubbabel, Zerubbabel the father of Abihud, Abihud the father of Eliakim, Eliakim the father of Azor, Azor the father of Zadok, Zadok the father of Akim, Akim the father of Elihud, Elihud the father of Eleazar, Eleazar the father of Matthan,

> *Matthan the father of Jacob, and Jacob the father of, the husband of Mary, and Mary was the mother of Jesus who is called the Messiah.*
>
> *Thus, there were fourteen generations in all from Abraham to David, fourteen from David to the exile to Babylon, and fourteen from the exile to the Messiah.*
>
> *Matthew 1:1-17*
New International Version (NIV)

Jacob - Often, we struggle to be obedient to God just as Jacob, the son of Isaac, struggled with obeying God throughout his life. Through many of his struggles, he began to mature in his faith in God, and thus, Jacob became a true servant of God. Jacobs fighting with God meant he missed out on many blessings; therefore, the sooner we trust in God, the sooner we will benefit from His blessings.

The covenant in Genesis 28:13-15 promises possession of land, multiple offspring, and blessings. In Genesis 25:29-34, Jacob receives his inheritance from his father, Isaac, which is usually reserved for the firstborn. Esau surrendered his birthright at a time when he was famished and wanted something to eat. Jacob made Esau promise with an oath to exchange his birthright for red stew to eat.

> *And behold, the Lord stood above it and said, "I am the Lord, the God of Abraham your father and the God of Isaac. The land on which you lie I will give to you and to your offspring. Your offspring shall be like the dust*

> *of the earth, and you shall spread abroad to the west and to the east and to the north and to the south, and in you and your offspring shall all the families of the earth be blessed. Behold, I am with you and will keep you wherever you go, and will bring you back to this land. For I will not leave you until I have done what I have promised you."*
>
> *Genesis 28: 13-15*
> *English Standard Version (ESV)*

> *Once when Jacob was cooking some stew, Esau came in from the open country, famished. He said to Jacob, "Quick, let me have some of that red stew! I'm famished!" (Esau was also called Edom, Edom means "red", because he was born red all over.) Jacob replied, "First sell me your birthright." "Look, I am about to die," Esau said. "What good is the birthright to me?" But Jacob said, "Swear to me first." So he swore an oath to him, selling his birthright to Jacob.*
>
> *Genesis 25:29-34*
> *New International Version(NIV)*

In each of these covenants, God's promises are contingent on obedience to His commands. When we are obedient to God, we are demonstrating our love, trust, and faith in Him. Various scriptures that command us to walk in obedience so that we may have a long life and be prosperous are found in Deuteronomy 5:33, Jeremiah 7:23, Ephesians 6:1-3, Luke 11:29, and James 1:25.

Walk in obedience to all that the Lord your God has commanded you, so that you may live and prosper and prolong your days in the land that you will possess.

Deuteronomy 5:33
New International Version (NIV)

But I gave them this command: Obey me, and I will be your God and you will be my people. Walk in obedience to all I command you, that it may go well with you.

Jeremiah 7:23
New International Version (NIV)

Children, obey your parents in the Lord, for this is right. "Honor your father and mother"— which is the first commandment with a promise— "so that it may go well with you and that you may enjoy long life on the earth."

Ephesians 6:1-3
New International Version (NIV)

He replied, "Blessed rather are those who hear the word of God and obey it."

Luke 11:29
New International Version (NIV)

But whoever looks intently into the perfect law that gives freedom, and continues in it—not

> *forgetting what they have heard, but doing it—they will be blessed in what they do.*
> *James 1:25*
> *New International Version (NIV)*

Disobedience brought punishment, calamity, and death. Here are a couple of verses found in Proverbs 1:23-33 and Leviticus 26:14-39.

> *But since you refuse to listen when I call and no one pays attention when I stretch out my hand, since you disregard all my advice and do not accept my rebuke, I in turn will laugh when disaster strikes you; I will mock when calamity overtakes you — when calamity overtakes you like a storm, when disaster sweeps over you like a whirlwind, when distress and trouble overwhelm you.*
>
> *"Then they will call to me but I will not answer; they will look for me but will not find me, since they hated knowledge and did not choose to fear the Lord.*
>
> *Since they would not accept my advice and spurned my rebuke, they will eat the fruit of their ways and be filled with the fruit of their schemes. For the waywardness of the simple will kill them, and the complacency of fools will destroy them; but whoever listens to me will live in safety and be at ease, without fear of harm."*
> *Proverbs 1:23-33*
> *New International Version (NIV)*

Punishment for Disobedience

"'But if you will not listen to me and carry out all these commands, and if you reject my decrees and abhor my laws and fail to carry out all my commands and so violate my covenant, then I will do this to you: I will bring on you sudden terror, wasting diseases and fever that will destroy your sight and sap your strength. You will plant seed in vain, because your enemies will eat it. I will set my face against you so that you will be defeated by your enemies; those who hate you will rule over you, and you will flee even when no one is pursuing you.

"'If after all this you will not listen to me, I will punish you for your sins seven times over. I will break down your stubborn pride and make the sky above you like iron and the ground beneath you like bronze. Your strength will be spent in vain, because your soil will not yield its crops, nor will the trees of your land yield their fruit.

"'If you remain hostile toward me and refuse to listen to me, I will multiply your afflictions seven times over, as your sins deserve. I will send wild animals against you, and they will rob you of your children, destroy your cattle and make you so few in number that your roads will be deserted.

"'If in spite of these things you do not accept my correction but continue to be hostile toward me, I myself will be hostile toward you and will afflict you for your sins seven times over. And I will bring the sword on you to avenge the breaking of the covenant. When you withdraw into your cities, I will send a plague among you, and you will be given into enemy hands. When I cut off your supply of bread, ten women will be able to bake your bread in one oven, and they will dole out the bread by weight. You will eat, but you will not be satisfied.

"'If in spite of this you still do not listen to me but continue to be hostile toward me, then in my anger I will be hostile toward you, and I myself will punish you for your sins seven times over. You will eat the flesh of your sons and the flesh of your daughters. I will destroy your high places, cut down your incense altars and pile your dead bodies on the lifeless forms of your idols, and I will abhor you. I will turn your cities into ruins and lay waste your sanctuaries, and I will take no delight in the pleasing aroma of your offerings. I myself will lay waste the land, so that your enemies who live there will be appalled. I will scatter you among the nations and will draw out my sword and pursue you. Your land will be laid waste, and your cities will lie in ruins. Then the land will enjoy its sabbath years all the

time that it lies desolate and you are in the country of your enemies; then the land will rest and enjoy its sabbaths. All the time that it lies desolate, the land will have the rest it did not have during the sabbaths you lived in it.

"'As for those of you who are left, I will make their hearts so fearful in the lands of their enemies that the sound of a windblown leaf will put them to flight. They will run as though fleeing from the sword, and they will fall, even though no one is pursuing them. They will stumble over one another as though fleeing from the sword, even though no one is pursuing them. So you will not be able to stand before your enemies. You will perish among the nations; the land of your enemies will devour you. Those of you who are left will waste away in the lands of their enemies because of their sins; also because of their ancestors' sins they will waste away.

Leviticus 26:14-39
New International Version (NIV)

Deuteronomy 28:1-68 list blessings for obedience and curses for disobedience:

Blessings for Obedience

If you fully obey the Lord your God and carefully follow all his commands I give you today, the Lord your God will set you high above all the nations on earth. All these blessings will come on you and accompany you if you obey the Lord your God: You will be blessed in the city and blessed in the country.

The fruit of your womb will be blessed, and the crops of your land and the young of your livestock—the calves of your herds and the lambs of your flocks.

Your basket and your kneading trough will be blessed. You will be blessed when you come in and blessed when you go out. The Lord will grant that the enemies who rise up against you will be defeated before you. They will come at you from one direction but flee from you in seven. The Lord will send a blessing on your barns and on everything you put your hand to. The Lord your God will bless you in the land he is giving you. The Lord will establish you as his holy people, as he promised you on oath, if you keep the commands of the Lord your God and walk in obedience to him. Then all the peoples on earth will see that you are called by the name of the Lord, and they will fear you. The Lord will grant you abundant prosperity—in the fruit of your womb, the young of your livestock and the crops of your ground—in the land he swore to your ancestors to give you.

The Lord will open the heavens, the storehouse of his bounty, to send rain on your land in season and to bless all the work of your hands. You will lend to many nations but will borrow from none. The Lord will make you the head, not the tail. If you pay attention to the commands of the Lord your God that I give you this day and carefully follow them, you will always be at the top, never at the bottom. Do not turn aside from any of the commands I give you today, to the right or to the left, following other gods and serving them.

Curses for Disobedience

However, if you do not obey the Lord your God and do not carefully follow all his commands and decrees I am giving you today, all these curses will come on you and overtake you: You will be cursed in the city and cursed in the country.

Your basket and your kneading trough will be cursed. The fruit of your womb will be cursed, and the crops of your land, and the calves of your herds and the lambs of your flocks. You will be cursed when you come in and cursed when you go out. The Lord will send on you curses, confusion and rebuke in everything you put your hand to, until you are destroyed and come to sudden ruin because of the evil you have done in forsaking him. The Lord will plague you with diseases until he has destroyed you from the land you are entering to possess. The Lord will strike you with wasting disease, with fever and inflammation, with scorching heat and drought, with blight and mildew, which will plague you until you perish. The sky over your head will be bronze, the ground beneath you iron. The Lord will turn the rain of your country into dust and powder; it will come down from the skies until you are destroyed. The Lord will cause you to be defeated before your enemies. You will come at them from one direction but flee from them in seven, and you will become a thing of horror to all the kingdoms on earth. Your carcasses will be food for all the birds and the wild animals, and there will be no one to frighten them away. The Lord will afflict you with the boils of Egypt and with tumors, festering sores and the itch, from which you cannot be cured. The Lord will afflict you with madness, blindness and confusion of mind. At midday you will grope about like a blind person in the dark. You will be unsuccessful in everything you do; day after day you will be oppressed and robbed, with no one to rescue you. You will be pledged to be married to a woman, but another will take her and rape her. You will build a house, but you will not live in it. You will plant a vineyard, but you will not even begin to enjoy its fruit. Your ox will be slaughtered before your eyes, but you will eat none of it. Your donkey will be forcibly taken from you and will not be returned. Your sheep will be given to your enemies, and no one will rescue them. Your sons and daughters will be given to another nation, and you will wear out your eyes watching for them day after day, powerless to lift a hand. A people that you do not know will eat what your land and labor produce, and you will have nothing but cruel oppression all your days. The sights you see will drive you mad. The Lord will afflict your knees and legs with painful boils that cannot be cured, spreading from the soles of your feet to the top of your head. The Lord will drive you and the king you set over you to a nation unknown to you or your ancestors. There you will worship other gods, gods of wood and stone. You will become a thing of horror, a byword and an object of ridicule among all the peoples where the Lord will drive you. You will sow much seed in the field but you will harvest little, because locusts will devour it. You will plant vineyards and cultivate them but you will not drink the wine or gather the grapes, because worms will eat them. You will have olive trees throughout your country but you will not use the oil, because the olives will drop off. You will have sons and daughters but you will not keep them, because they will go into captivity. Swarms of locusts will take over all your trees and the crops of your land. The foreigners who reside among you will rise above you higher and higher, but you will sink lower and lower. They will lend to you, but you will not lend to them. They will be the head, but you will be the tail. All these curses will come on you. They will pursue you and overtake you until you are destroyed, because you did not obey the Lord your God and observe the commands and decrees he gave you. They will be a sign and a wonder to you and your descendants forever. Because you did not serve the Lord your God joyfully and gladly in the time of prosperity, therefore in hunger and thirst, in nakedness and dire poverty, you will serve the enemies the Lord sends against you. He will put an iron yoke on your neck until he has destroyed you. The Lord will bring a nation against you from far away, from the ends of the earth, like an swooping down, a nation whose language you will not understand, a fierce-looking nation without respect for the old or pity for the young. They will devour the young of your livestock and the crops of your land until you are destroyed. They will leave you no grain, new wine or olive oil, nor any calves of your herds or lambs of your flocks until you are ruined. They will lay siege to all the cities throughout your land until the high fortified walls in which you trust fall down. They will besiege all the cities throughout the land the Lord your God is giving you. Because of the suffering your enemy will inflict on you during the siege, you will eat the fruit of the womb, the flesh of the sons and daughters the Lord your God has given you. Even the most gentle and sensitive man among you will have no compassion on his own brother or the wife he loves or his surviving children, and he will not give to one of them any of the flesh of his children that he is eating. It will be all he has left because of the suffering your enemy will inflict on you during the siege of all your cities. The most gentle and sensitive woman among you—so sensitive and gentle that she would not venture to touch the ground with the sole of her foot—will begrudge the husband she loves and her own son or daughter the afterbirth from her womb and the children she bears. For in her dire need she intends to eat them secretly because of the suffering your enemy will inflict on you during the siege of your cities. If you do not carefully follow all the words of this law, which are written in this book, and do not revere this glorious and awesome name —the Lord your God— the Lord will send fearful plagues on you and your descendants, harsh and prolonged disasters, and severe and lingering illnesses. He will bring on you all the diseases of Egypt that you dreaded, and they will cling to you. The Lord will also bring on you every kind of sickness and disaster not recorded in this Book of the Law, until you are destroyed. You who were as numerous as the stars in the sky will be left but few in number, because you did not obey the Lord your God. Just as it pleased the Lord to make you prosper and increase in number, so it will please him to ruin and destroy you. You will be uprooted from the land you are entering to possess. Then the Lord will scatter you among all nations, from one end of the earth to the other. There you will worship other gods—gods of wood and stone, which neither you nor your ancestors have known. Among those nations you will find no repose, no resting place for the sole of your foot. There the Lord will give you an anxious mind, eyes weary with longing, and a despairing heart. You will live in constant suspense, filled with dread both night and day, never sure of your life. In the morning you will say, "If only it were evening!" and in the evening, "If only it were morning!"— because of the terror that will fill your hearts and the sights that your eyes will see. The Lord will send you back in ships to Egypt on a journey I said you should never make again. There you will offer yourselves for sale to your enemies as male and female slaves, but no one will buy you.

Deuteronomy 28:1-68
New International Version (NIV)

- The Mosaic Covenant

The Israelites had relocated from Canaan to Egypt because Joseph was there, and he was able to provide for them during the time of famine. However, with the rising of a new Pharaoh, the Israelites were turned into slaves and were made to work hard and for long hours. Therefore, the Israelites cried out to God, and God heard their cry, as stated in Exodus 2:34. God remembered his covenant with Abraham, Isaac, and Jacob, and God led them out of Egypt with power and a mighty hand, as stated in Exodus 32:11.

> *God heard their groaning and he remembered his covenant with Abraham, with Isaac and with Jacob.*
>
> *Exodus 2:34*
> *New International Version (NIV)*

> *But Moses sought the favor of the Lord his God. "Lord," he said, "why should your anger burn against your people, whom you brought out of Egypt with great power and a mighty hand?*
>
> *Exodus 32:11*
> *New International Version (NIV)*

God chose Moses to lead His people from Egypt to the Promised Land; this is found in Exodus 3:6-10.

> *Then he said, "I am the God of your father, the God of Abraham, the God of Isaac and*

> *the God of Jacob." At this, Moses hid his face, because he was afraid to look at God. The Lord said, "I have indeed seen the misery of my people in Egypt. I have heard them crying out because of their slave drivers, and I am concerned about their suffering. So I have come down to rescue them from the hand of the Egyptians and to bring them up out of that land into a good and spacious land, a land flowing with milk and honey —the home of the Canaanites, Hittites, Amorites, Perizzites, Hivites and Jebusites. And now the cry of the Israelites has reached me, and I have seen the way the Egyptians are oppressing them. So now, go. I am sending you to Pharaoh to bring my people the Israelites out of Egypt."*
> *Exodus 3:6-10*
> *New International Version (NIV)*

While on their journey to the Promised Land, God gave Moses His Divine law while on Mount Sinai, the *Ten Commandments*, which are God's Laws versus Moses' Law.

In the article from <u>Preparing For Eternity</u>, *Moses' Law vs. God's Ten Commandments* is described as follows:

> Moses' law was the temporary, ceremonial law of the Old Testament. It regulated the priesthood, sacrifices, rituals, meat and drink offerings, etc., all of which foreshadowed the cross. This law was added "till the seed should come," and

that seed was Christ (Galatians 3:16, 19). The ritual and ceremony of Moses' law pointed toward Christ's sacrifice. When He died, this law came to an end, but the Ten Commandments (God's law) "stand forever and ever." Psalm 111:7-8.[9]

The promises were spoken to Abraham and to his seed. Scripture does not say "and to seeds," meaning many people, but "and to your seed," meaning one person, who is Christ.

Galatians 3:16
New International Version (NIV)

Why, then, was the law given at all? It was added because of transgressions until the Seed to whom the promise referred had come. The law was given through angels and entrusted to a mediator.

Galatians 3:19
New International Version (NIV)

The works of his hands are faithful and just; all his precepts are trustworthy. They are established for ever and ever, enacted in faithfulness and uprightness.

Psalm 111:7-8
New International Version (NIV)

---

[9] https://www.preparingforeternity.com/mosevs10.htm

Thus, the Mosaic Covenant was a temporary covenant for the Israelites well-being as God had promised that a new covenant was forthcoming that would be for all mankind. This is found in Jeremiah 31:31-34.

> *"The days are coming," declares the Lord, "when I will make a new covenant with the people of Israel and with the people of Judah. It will not be like the covenant I made with their ancestors when I took them by the hand to lead them out of Egypt, because they broke my covenant, though I was a husband to them," declares the Lord. "This is the covenant I will make with the people of Israel after that time," declares the Lord. "I will put my law in their minds and write it on their hearts. I will be their God, and they will be my people.*
>
> *Jeremiah 31:31-34*
> *New International Version (NIV)*

- The New Covenant

In previous covenants, the Israelites were obligatory to strict obedience to God by keeping the Mosaic Law. They were required to sacrifice animals at different times based on ritual and purpose. For example, the Day of Atonement was celebrated once a year to cover the penalty for the sins of the Israelites. This was a temporary covering, and a reminder of their sins since the old covenants did not provide a way to take away sins; see Hebrews 10:1-4.

> *The law is only a shadow of the good things that are coming—not the realities themselves. For this reason it can never, by the same sacrifices repeated endlessly year after year, make perfect those who draw near to worship. Otherwise, would they not have stopped being offered? For the worshipers would have been cleansed once for all, and would no longer have felt guilty for their sins. But those sacrifices are an annual reminder of sins. It is impossible for the blood of bulls and goats to take away sins.*
>
> *Hebrews 10:1-4*
> *New International Version (NIV)*

Animal sacrifice was necessary to remind them of the seriousness of sin. In Hebrews 9:22, the law required everything to be cleaned with blood because without the shedding of blood, there was no forgiveness.

> *In fact, the law requires that nearly everything be cleansed with blood, and without the shedding of blood there is no forgiveness.*
> *Hebrews 9:22*
> *New International Version (NIV)*

The announcement of the New Covenant was foretold by Moses, Jeremiah, Ezekiel, and Jesus. This is found in Jeremiah 31:31-34 (see above) and Ezekiel 36:26-27. In Matthew 5:17, Jesus announced that he came to establish a New Covenant and not to abolish the old laws but to fulfill them.

> *And I will give you a new heart, and a new spirit I will put within you. And I will remove the heart of stone from your flesh and give you a heart of flesh. And I will put my Spirit within you, and cause you to walk in my statutes and be careful to obey my rules.*
>
> *Ezekiel 36:26-27*
> *English Standard Version (ESV)*

> *Do not think that I have come to abolish the Law or the Prophets; I have not come to abolish them but to fulfill them.*
>
> *Matthew 5:17*
> *New International Version (NIV)*

Under the New Covenant, the need for animal sacrifice ended since we were made holy through the sacrifice Jesus made when He was crucified. In the old covenant, only the High Priest was allowed to yearly enter the Holy of Holies on Yom Kippur to offer blood sacrifices and incense in the presence of God. Yom Kippur means "Day of Atonement" and refers to the annual Jewish observance of fasting, prayer, and repentance.[10]

But now our High Priest is Jesus Christ, our perfect and final sacrifice for all mankind. In Hebrews 4:14-16, Hebrews 2:17, Hebrews 7:26-27, and Hebrews 9:12, the scriptures inform us that Jesus Christ is the High Priest.

---

[10] https://reformjudaism.org/jewish-holidays/yom-kippur-day-atonement

Therefore, since we have a great high priest who has ascended into heaven, Jesus the Son of God, let us hold firmly to the faith we profess. For we do not have a high priest who is unable to empathize with our weaknesses, but we have one who has been tempted in every way, just as we are —yet he did not sin. Let us then approach God's throne of grace with confidence, so that we may receive mercy and find grace to help us in our time of need.
Hebrews 4:14-16
New International Version (NIV)

For this reason he had to be made like them, fully human in every way, in order that he might become a merciful and faithful high priest in service to God, and that he might make atonement for the sins of the people.
Hebrews 2:17
New International Version (NIV)

Such a high priest truly meets our need—one who is holy, blameless, pure, set apart from sinners, exalted above the heavens. Unlike the other high priests, he does not need to offer sacrifices day after day, first for his own sins, and then for the sins of the people. He sacrificed for their sins once for all when he offered himself.
Hebrews 7:26-27
New International Version (NIV)

> *He did not enter by means of the blood of goats and calves; but he entered the Most Holy Place once for all by his own blood, thus obtaining eternal redemption.*
>
> *Hebrews 9:12*
> New International Version (NIV)

In Luke 22:20, Jesus foretold the disciples of His death on the cross and also told them that the New Covenant is forthcoming. This covenant opened the door for a personal relationship with God and man through Jesus Christ as our mediator. The requirement is to wholeheartedly declare in the belief of Jesus Christ as the Messiah, the Savior for all mankind. With this, our sins are forgiven, we have the assurance of eternal salvation, and we become co-heirs with Jesus Christ, see Romans 8:16-17, Galatians 3:26-28, Galatians 4:7, and John 1:12.

> *In the same way, after the supper he took the cup, saying, "This cup is the new covenant in my blood, which is poured out for you.*
>
> *Luke 22:20*
> *New International Version (NIV)*

> *The Spirit himself testifies with our spirit that we are God's children.*
>
> *Now if we are children, then we are heirs—heirs of God and co-heirs with Christ, if indeed we share in his sufferings in order that we may also share in his glory.*
>
> *Romans 8:16-17*
> *New International Version (NIV)*

So in Christ Jesus you are all children of God through faith, for all of you who were baptized into Christ have clothed yourselves with Christ. There is neither Jew nor Gentile, neither slave nor free, nor is there male and female, for you are all one in Christ Jesus.

Galatians 3:26-28
New International Version (NIV)

So you are no longer a slave, but God's child; and since you are his child, God has made you also an heir.

Galatians 4:7
New International Version (NIV)

Yet to all who did receive him, to those who believed in his name, he gave the right to become children of God —

John 1:12
New International Version (NIV)

CHAPTER 3

God's Promise

The Bible is filled with many promises for those that follow the teachings found in the scriptures; that is, we are to love the Lord with all our heart, soul, and mind and love our neighbor as ourselves. Likewise, there are many verses for those that do not follow the teaching recorded in the Bible. Here are a few promises that Christians can enjoy while seeking God.

- God's Peace

With a total commitment to loving and serving the Lord, we can experience God's peace. Believing in the death and resurrection of Jesus, believing that our sins have been forgiven, and Jesus paid the price for our sins, allow us to seek His presence and bask in His peace. There are two virtues needed to produce peace; justice, which is showing respect for people and not engaging in conflict whenever possible, and righteousness, which is living a life pleasing to God. When justice prevails and is ruled by righteousness, people can live in harmony and peace. A total commitment means we must put our trust in God even in times of adversity, knowing He is working for the good of all who call upon Him. We don't want to assume that everything will go our way because then we will set ourselves up for disappointments, but instead stay steadfast and in peace knowing God knows all and is working for our benefit.

Jealous, hurtful, and mean people can create havoc by throwing glitches in our lives that can cause stress and discouragement, but the longer I live and experience times of peace while going through adversity, I often wonder, "How can people cope without God's peace"?

Got Questions defines Peace as:

> *Peace is a state of tranquility or quietness of spirit that transcends circumstances. The term peace is described in Scripture as a gift from God and congruent with His character*[11]

Question: "What is the peace of God, and how can I experience it?"

> Answer: Philippians 4:7 refers to "the peace of God which transcends all understanding." Most of Paul's letters began with the words "Grace and peace to you from God our Father and the Lord Jesus Christ." Peace is a state of tranquility or quietness of spirit that transcends circumstances. The term peace is

---

[11] https://www.gotquestions.org/peace-of-God.html

described in Scripture as a gift from God and congruent with His character.[12]

And the peace of God, which transcends all understanding, will guard your hearts and your minds in Christ Jesus.

Philippians 4:7
New International Version (NIV)

May God himself, the God of peace, sanctify you through and through. May your whole spirit, soul and body be kept blameless at the coming of our Lord Jesus Christ.

1 Thessalonians 5:23
New International Version (NIV)

Peace and mercy to all who follow this rule—to the Israel of God

Galatians 6:16
New International Version (NIV)

Who have been chosen according to the foreknowledge of God the Father, through the sanctifying work of the Spirit, to be obedient to Jesus Christ and sprinkled with his blood: Grace and peace be yours in abundance.

1 Peter 1:2
New International Version (NIV)

---

[12] https://www.gotquestions.org/peace-of-God.html

> *Now may the God of peace, who through the blood of the eternal covenant brought back from the dead our Lord Jesus, that great Shepherd of the sheep, equip you with everything good for doing his will.*
>
> *Hebrews 13:20*
> *New International Version (NIV)*

- Peace Like a River

We will experience God's peace like a flowing river when we are obedient, and when we set our mind on Him, trust and lean on Jesus wholeheartedly and steadfastly. This peace is a spiritual blessing in Christ just as God promises us salvation and strength through Jesus Christ, He promises forgiveness of sins when we repent and seek guidance for daily living encompassed with His peace. Peace, like a river, is the presence of the Lord even in times of trials and tribulations. When I first think of peace like a river, the word tranquility comes to mind. I mentally see a continuously flowing river of freshwater slowly running across a long, curvy, calm, and peaceful stream, an image of God's glorious creation. Isaiah 66:12 promises peace like a river and wealth of nations like a flooding stream:

> *For this is what the Lord says: "I will extend peace to her like a river, and the wealth of nations like a flooding stream; you will nurse and be carried on her arm and dandled on her knees.*
>
> *Isaiah 66:12*
> *New International Version (NIV)*

Here is an example of steadfast trusting in God. While in a flight, the turbulence was frightful as the airplane bounced around with drops and lifts similar to a roller coaster ride. But as I began to pray, I felt the peace of God and His presence. I trusted in Him and acknowledged to myself that no matter what happened, He was in control. Later I learned that planes usually do not crash due to turbulence. It was a good thing that I trusted in God and did not rely on my understanding, see Proverbs 3:5, or else I would have worried for nothing.

> *Trust in the Lord with all your heart and lean not on your own understanding; in all your ways submit to him, and he will make your paths straight.*
>
> *Proverbs 3:5 (NIV)*
> New International Version

According to Forbes: *Can Turbulence Cause a Plane to Crash?*

> No, normal turbulence that aircraft experience will typically not cause an aircraft to "crash" for two reasons.
>
> 1. Most turbulence is well within what aircraft are designed to fly through.
> 2. For moderate or extreme turbulence, pilots are trained to slow the aircraft down to the appropriate "maneuvering speed" for the aircraft's current weight. This protects the aircraft in such a way that if it encounters extreme turbulence, the aircraft wings will

> essentially "stall" before the aircraft is damaged. The concept of "stall" in this case doesn't mean the pilot loses control; it's simply a design feature that protects the aircraft's structure.[13]

Isaiah 48:18, Isaiah 26:3-4, John 14:27, and John 16:33 remind us to be steadfast and trust in the Lord forever. Then we will receive His peace like a river, and our righteousness will be like the waves of the sea.

> *Oh that you had paid attention to my commandments! Then your peace would have been like a river, and your righteousness like the waves of the sea.*
>
> Isaiah 48:18
> English Standard Version (ESV)

> *You will keep in perfect peace those whose minds are steadfast, because they trust in you. Trust in the Lord forever.*
>
> Isaiah 26: 3-4
> New International Version (NIV)

> *Peace I leave with you; my peace I give you. I do not give to you as the world gives. Do not let your hearts be troubled and do not be afraid.*
>
> John 14:27
> New International Version (NIV)

---

[13] https://www.forbes.com/sites/quora/2018/01/03/can-turbulence-cause-a-plane-to-crash/#f2a69b67680f

> *"I have told you these things, so that in me you may have peace. In this world you will have trouble. But take heart! I have overcome the world."*
>
> *John 16:33*
> *New International Version (NIV)*

- Help in Times of Anxiety

Philippians 4:5-9 reflects on the promise of the peace of God when putting one's trust in Jesus Christ and seeking righteousness. We are instructed not to be anxious about anything but pray with a thankful heart. Anxiety for the future results from our lack of trust in the Lord and putting trust in ourselves and focusing on worldly things. Worldly thing is described in 1 John 2:15-17 as the lust of the flesh, lust of the eyes, and the pride of life. Anxiety comes with a price as this can lead to physical and mental problems such as depression, worry, fear, and heart problems; thus, we are to cast all our cares on Jesus and not worry. We are also instructed not to worry about tomorrow as to what we will eat or wear. Be content and not compare ourselves with others, because God will take care of our needs. God knows exactly what is needed, and He provides generously (see Philippians 4:19). 1 Peter 5:7 pertains to anxiety, casting our cares on Jesus and not worrying. Once we give the Lord our burdens by trusting in Him, then we may experience a feeling like a heavy load has been lifted off our shoulders.

> *Let your gentleness be evident to all. The Lord is near. Do not be anxious about anything,*

but in every situation, by prayer and petition, with thanksgiving, present your requests to God. And the peace of God, which transcends all understanding, will guard your hearts and your minds in Christ Jesus. Finally, brothers and sisters, whatever is true, whatever is noble, whatever is right, whatever is pure, whatever is lovely, whatever is admirable—if anything is excellent or praiseworthy—think about such things. Whatever you have learned or received or heard from me, or seen in me—put it into practice. And the God of peace will be with you.

Philippians 4:5-9
New International Version (NIV)

Do not love the world or anything in the world. If anyone loves the world, love for the Father is not in them. For everything in the world—the lust of the flesh, the lust of the eyes, and the pride of life—comes not from the Father but from the world. The world and its desires pass away, but whoever does the will of God lives forever.

1 John 2:15-17
New International Version (NIV)

And my God will meet all your needs according to the riches of his glory in Christ Jesus.

Philippians 4:19
New International Version (NIV)

Cast all your anxiety on him because he cares for you.

1 Peter 5:7
New International Version (NIV)

"Therefore, I tell you, do not worry about your life, what you will eat or drink; or about your body, what you will wear. Is not life more than food, and the body more than clothes? Look at the birds of the air; they do not sow or reap or store away in barns, and yet your heavenly Father feeds them. Are you not much more valuable than they? Can any one of you by worrying add a single hour to your life? "And why do you worry about clothes? See how the flowers of the field grow. They do not labor or spin. Yet I tell you that not even Solomon in all his splendor was dressed like one of these. If that is how God clothes the grass of the field, which is here today and tomorrow is thrown into the fire, will he not much more clothe you—you of little faith? So do not worry, saying, 'What shall we eat?' or 'What shall we drink?' or 'What shall we wear?' For the pagans run after all these things, and your heavenly Father knows that you need them. But seek first his kingdom and his righteousness, and all these things will be given to you as well. Therefore do not worry about tomorrow, for tomorrow will worry

> *about itself. Each day has enough trouble of its own.*
>
> *Matthew 6:25-34*
> *New International Version (NIV)*

- Help in Time of Temptation

With a genuine love for others, one will demonstrate their love by encouraging one another to live in righteousness and to walk away from a worldly lifestyle. This is exactly what God did when He demonstrated His love when we were still sinners; He sacrificed His only begotten son, Jesus Christ. Jesus came to earth in human form, ministered to everyone along His journey, lived as a servant, and as the best example we have for living in righteousness. Jesus was tempted but refused the devil's tricks by responding with words found in the scriptures. In Hebrews 4:15, we are told that Jesus was tempted in every way that we are, but He did not sin. In 1 Corinthians 10:13, God in His faithfulness does not allow one to be tempted beyond one's capabilities, but when tempted, He will provide a way of escape. This means that when tempted, God wants us to depend on Him for help. He promises not to abandon us because we cannot handle the tough times alone. In Psalm 16:10-11, God will not abandon us even in death because He will take us to our heavenly home. Jesus was crucified for all our sins, even though He was sinless since it was the only way to fully pay for our sins. In 1 Peter 2:22, St. Peter stated that Jesus was sinless; Jesus submitted to authority both to His Heavenly Father and earthly authority. Unlike all humanity, Jesus' sinlessness is supported in Romans 3:23-24, 1John 1:8, 1John 3:5, 2 Corinthians 5:21, and Isaiah 53:9.

> *For we do not have a high priest who is unable to empathize with our weaknesses, but we have one who has been tempted in every way, just as we are —yet he did not sin.*
> *Hebrews 4:15*
> *New International Version (NIV)*

> *No temptation has overtaken you except what is common to mankind. And God is faithful; he will not let you be tempted beyond what you can bear. But when you are tempted, he will also provide a way out so that you can endure it.*
> *1 Corinthians 10:13*
> *New International Version (NIV)*

> *Because you will not abandon me to the realm of the dead, nor will you let your faithful one see decay. You make known to me the path of life; you will fill me with joy in your presence, with eternal pleasures at your right hand.*
> *Psalm 16:10-11*
> *New International Version (NIV)*

"He committed no sin, and no deceit was found in his mouth."

1 Peter 2:22
New International Version (NIV)

For all have sinned and fall short of the glory of God, and all are justified freely by his grace through the redemption that came by Christ Jesus.

Romans 3:23-24
New International Version (NIV)

If we claim to be without sin, we deceive ourselves and the truth is not in us.

1 John 1:8
New International Version (NIV)

But you know that he appeared so that he might take away our sins. And in him is no sin.

1 John 3:5
New International Version (NIV)

God made him who had no sin to be sin for us, so that in him we might become the righteousness of God.

2 Corinthians 5:21
New International Version (NIV)

He was assigned a grave with the wicked, and with the rich in his death, though he had

> *done no violence, nor was any deceit in his mouth.*
>
> *Isaiah 53:9*
> *New International Version (NIV)*

- Jesus the Only Mediator to God the Father

With the crucifixion and resurrection, our risen Savior was given the special place of honor, seated at the right hand of God the Father. Because Jesus was willing and was obedient to God, God exalted Jesus to the highest position and gave him the name that is above every name, Colossians 3:1 and Philippians 2:6-11.

> *Set your hearts on things above, where Christ is, seated at the right hand of God.*
>
> Colossians 3:1
> New International Version (NIV)

> *Who, being in very nature God, did not consider equality with God something to be used to his own advantage; rather, he made himself nothing by taking the very nature of a servant, being made in human likeness. And being found in appearance as a man, he humbled himself by becoming obedient to death—even death on a cross! Therefore, God exalted him to the highest place and gave him the name that is above every name, that at the name of Jesus every knee should bow, in heaven and on earth and under the earth,*

> *and every tongue acknowledge that Jesus Christ is Lord, to the glory of God the Father.*
> *Philippians 2:6-11*
> *New International Version (NIV)*

Along with the inheritance of sin, which came from the fall of Adam, the need for a savior was imminent since we cannot save ourselves. In Roman 3:10, we are reminded that there is not even one righteous person. Therefore, the only punishment for our sins would be eternal death, which is found in Romans 6:23. Jesus is the only one who could fulfill the position as our mediator to the Father. Without Jesus, there would be no hope because sin keeps us away from God as God hates sin.

> *As it is written: "There is no one righteous, not even one.*
>
> *Romans 3:10*
> *New International Version (NIV)*

> *For the wages of sin is death, but the gift of God is eternal life in Christ Jesus our Lord.*
> *Romans 6:23*
> *New International Version (NIV)*

The only way to pay for our sin would be through the blood of Jesus, the final sacrificial atonement. The meaning of Atonement, according to, is:

> *In Christianity, atonement refers to the needed reconciliation between sinful mankind and the holy God. This reconciliation is possible*

> *through the atoning sacrifice of Jesus Christ, as expressed in Romans 3:25, Romans 5:11, and Romans 5:19. Atonement is the Bible's central message.*[14]
>
> *God presented Christ as a sacrifice of atonement, through the shedding of his blood —to be received by faith. He did this to demonstrate his righteousness, because in his forbearance he had left the sins committed beforehand unpunished.*
>
> Romans 3:25
New International Version (NIV)
>
> *Not only is this so, but we also boast in God through our Lord Jesus Christ, through whom we have now received reconciliation.*
>
> Romans 5:11
New International Version (NIV)
>
> *For just as through the disobedience of the one man the many were made sinners, so also through the obedience of the one man the many will be made righteous.*
>
> Romans 5:19
New International Version (NIV)

As a mediator, Jesus' representation can be paralleled somewhat to the duties performed by an attorney. The

---

[14] https://www.christianity.com/wiki/salvation/what-is-atonement-biblical-meaning-and-definition.html

attorney will plead a case of innocence or leniency on our behalf. However, when we accept Jesus, He will defend us, saying he has paid the debt for our sins allowing us to enter the Kingdom of God and receive eternal salvation. Here are a few verses confirming that Jesus is the only mediator to the Father: 1 Timothy 2:5. John 14:6, John 10-9, and John 3:16.

> *For there is one God and one mediator between God and mankind, the man Christ Jesus.*
>
> *1 Timothy 2:5*
> *New International Version (NIV)*

> *Jesus answered, "I am the way and the truth and the life. No one comes to the Father except through me.*
>
> *John 14:6*
> *New International Version (NIV)*

> *I am the gate; whoever enters through me will be saved.*
>
> *John 10:9*
> *New International Version (NIV)*

> *For God so loved the world that he gave his one and only Son, that whoever believes in him shall not perish but have eternal life.*
>
> *John 3:16*
> *New International Version (NIV)*

- God Protects

God protects and watches over His children like a shepherd who watches over his sheep. In John 10:10-13, Jesus states he is not like a hired hand that does not protect the sheep when fear of danger arises. Jesus' love for his sheep is genuine as He cares for His own and will stay to protect them. In John 10:14-15, Jesus is the good shepherd whom the sheep know, and He lays down his life for the sheep.

> *The thief comes only to steal and kill and destroy; I have come that they may have life, and have it to the full. "I am the good shepherd. The good shepherd lays down his life for the sheep. The hired hand is not the shepherd and does not own the sheep. So, when he sees the wolf coming, he abandons the sheep and runs away. Then the wolf attacks the flock and scatters it. The man runs away because he is a hired hand and cares nothing for the sheep.*
>
> *John 10:10-13*
> *New International Version (NIV)*

> *"For this is what the Sovereign Lord says: I myself will search for my sheep and look after them. As a shepherd looks after his scattered flock when he is with them, so will I look after my sheep. I will rescue them from all the places where they were scattered on a day of clouds and darkness. I will bring them out from the*

nations and gather them from the countries, and I will bring them into their own land. I will pasture them on the mountains of Israel, in the ravines and in all the settlements in the land. I will tend them in a good pasture, and the mountain heights of Israel will be their grazing land. There they will lie down in good grazing land, and there they will feed in a rich pasture on the mountains of Israel. I myself will tend my sheep and have them lie down, declares the Sovereign Lord.

Ezekiel 34:11-15
New International Version (NIV)

"I am the good shepherd; I know my sheep and my sheep know me— just as the Father knows me and I know the Father —and I lay down my life for the sheep.

John 10:14-15
New International Version (NIV)

In Ezekiel 34:11-15, the message of the coming Messiah was foretold using the example of the good shepherd who gathers the lost sheep and tends to them. Psalm 23:1-6 describes how the Sovereign Lord searches and cares for those that follow Him; He leads them to green pastures, rescues, and protects them. In Isaiah 40:11, we see the Lord as a shepherd with compassion and caring as the Lord gathers the lambs in his arms close to his heart and gently leads those that have young ones.

The Lord is my shepherd, I lack nothing. He makes me lie down in green pastures, he leads me beside quiet waters, he refreshes my soul. He guides me along the right paths for his name's sake. Even though I walk through the darkest valley, I will fear no evil, for you are with me; your rod and your staff, they comfort me. You prepare a table before me in the presence of my enemies. You anoint my head with oil; my cup overflows. Surely your goodness and love will follow me all the days of my life, and I will dwell in the house of the Lord forever.

Psalm 23:1-6
New International Version (NIV)

He tends his flock like a shepherd: He gathers the lambs in his arms and carries them close to his heart; he gently leads those that have young.

Isaiah 40:11
New International Version (NIV)

- Care and Discipline for Our Good

God's love for His children is unconditional and wholehearted. He demonstrates this by taking care of us, and when needed, he disciplines us, just as a good parent would. Often God chastens or allows His children to endure trials and tribulations to draw His children's attention to His leading so they will not stumble and turn away from

God. When one continues to sin by turning their back on what is right, not willing to repent of their sins, or not turning away from a sinful lifestyle, God allows them to dig a pit and fall into it. Once in the trap of the evil one and wanting to get out, Christians will often call upon God and repent. At times, God allows His children to fall to strengthen them by taking away undue confidence. When successful, mankind takes all the credit for their success and forgets that the blessings were because of the mercy and grace given by God. When our guard is down, Satan will attack what one perceives to be their strength as the person will be vulnerable and be an easy prey.

In many cases, God will use sin to make his children stronger, as seen in Luke 22:31-34, Matthew 26:69-75, and Luke 22:61-62. Simon Peter, a strong follower and one of the early disciples of Jesus Christ, was considered as Jesus' closest friend. Though Peter was passionate and a leader, he often failed in his journey, but Jesus faithfully guided him. When Jesus was coming to the end of His earthly ministry, Peter denied knowing Jesus three times (Jesus predicted this). Once Peter realized what he had done, he went outside and cried bitterly. Peter's crying came as a result of sorrow for his sins, especially when he saw Jesus' face. When Jesus appeared after the resurrection, Peter was embarrassed. He had a hard time as he was not able to speak to Jesus. However, in John 21:15-17, Jesus reaffirmed Peter's relationship when Jesus questioned Peter three times, saying, "Do you love me?" and then He told Peter, "Feed my sheep." Recollecting Jesus' promise of forgiveness allowed Peter the courage to repent making him a devoted disciple.

Luke 22:31, Matthew 26:69-75, and Luke 22:61-62 is an excerpt of when Peter denied knowing Jesus:

> *Simon, Simon, Satan has asked to sift all of you as wheat. But I have prayed for you, Simon, that your faith may not fail. And when you have turned back, strengthen your brothers." But he replied, "Lord, I am ready to go with you to prison and to death." Jesus answered, "I tell you, Peter, before the rooster crows today, you will deny three times that you know me."*
> *Luke 22:31-34*
> *New International Version (NIV)*

> *Now Peter was sitting out in the courtyard, and a servant girl came to him. "You also were with Jesus of Galilee," she said. But he denied it before them all. "I don't know what you're talking about," he said. Then he went out to the gateway, where another servant girl saw him and said to the people there, "This fellow was with Jesus of Nazareth." He denied it again, with an oath: "I don't know the man!" After a little while, those standing there went up to Peter and said, "Surely you are one of them; your accent gives you away." Then he began to call down curses, and he swore to them, "I don't know the man!"*
>
> *Immediately a rooster crowed. Then Peter remembered the word Jesus had spoken: "Before the rooster crows, you will disown me*

three times." And he went outside and wept bitterly.

Matthew 26:69-75
New International Version (NIV)

The Lord turned and looked straight at Peter. Then Peter remembered the word the Lord had spoken to him: "Before the rooster crows today, you will disown me three times." And he went outside and wept bitterly.

Luke 22:61-62 (NIV)17
New International Version (NIV)

When they had finished eating, Jesus said to Simon Peter, "Simon son of John, do you love me more than these?" "Yes, Lord," he said, "you know that I love you." Jesus said, "Feed my lambs." Again Jesus said, "Simon son of John, do you love me?" He answered, "Yes, Lord, you know that I love you." Jesus said, "Take care of my sheep." The third time he said to him, "Simon son of John, do you love me?" Peter was hurt because Jesus asked him the third time, "Do you love me?" He said, "Lord, you know all things; you know that I love you." Jesus said, "Feed my sheep."

John 21:15-17
New International Version (NIV)

Many scriptures instruct us to discipline children for them to become honest, caring, and productive people. In some scriptures, we are instructed not to spare the rod while other scriptures do not refer to physical discipline. In any event, we are not to abuse or exasperate children; see Ephesians 6:4.

> *Fathers, do not exasperate your children; instead, bring them up in the training and instruction of the Lord.*
>
> *Ephesians 6:4*
> *New International Version (NIV)*

God's discipline is done in love to encourage us to become productive messengers of the Gospel of Jesus Christ, especially when taught at a young age. In Proverbs 22:6, we are to teach and bring up children so that when they get old, they will not turn away from God. God's instruction regarding disciplining children is found in Proverbs 22:6, Proverbs 23:13-14, Proverbs 22:15, Hebrews 12:5-11, Deuteronomy 8:5-6, Proverbs 10:17, and Proverbs 13:24:

> *Start children off on the way they should go, and even when they are old they will not turn from it.*
>
> *Proverbs 22:6*
> *New International Version (NIV)*

> *Do not withhold discipline from a child; if you punish them with the rod, they will not die. Punish them with the rod and save them from death.*
>
> *Proverbs 23:13-14*
> *New International Version (NIV)*

Folly is bound up in the heart of a child, but the rod of discipline will drive it far away.
Proverbs 22:15
New International Version (NIV)

And have you completely forgotten this word of encouragement that addresses you as a father addresses his son? It says, "My son, do not make light of the Lord's discipline, and do not lose heart when he rebukes you, because the Lord disciplines the one he loves, and he chastens everyone he accepts as his son."

Endure hardship as discipline; God is treating you as his children. For what children are not disciplined by their father? If you are not disciplined—and everyone undergoes discipline —then you are not legitimate, not true sons and daughters at all. Moreover, we have all had human fathers who disciplined us and we respected them for it. How much more should we submit to the Father of spirits and live! They disciplined us for a little while as they thought best; but God disciplines us for our good, in order that we may share in his holiness. No discipline seems pleasant at the time, but painful. Later on, however, it produces a harvest of righteousness and peace for those who have been trained by it
Hebrews 12:5-11
New International Version (NIV)

Know then in your heart that as a man disciplines his son, so the Lord your God disciplines you. Observe the commands of the Lord your God, walking in obedience to him and revering him.

Deuteronomy 8:5-6
New International Version (NIV)

Whoever heeds discipline shows the way to life, but whoever ignores correction leads others astray.

Proverbs 10: 17
New International Version (NIV)

Whoever spares the rod hates their children, but the one who loves their children is careful to discipline them.

Proverbs 13:24
New International Version (NIV)

- God's Mercy and Grace

In <u>All About God</u>, *God of Mercy explains Mercy and Grace:*

God of Mercy – Understanding Mercy

God is known to be a God of mercy and grace. Understanding mercy is often difficult for people as we tend to be a generation of "I'll get him for that" and "I hope they get what they deserve." Many have developed a nature of harsh criticism and want others to get what they have done to them and more. God, however, is merciful to even the worst offenders, sinners, and law-breakers. This means that even though He knows about our guilt, He doesn't always issue the punishment we deserved. To elaborate, the verse in Romans 3:23-24 says "…all have sinned and fall short of the glory of God, and are justified freely by His grace through the redemption that came by Jesus Christ."

Simply, we are all sinners and do not meet the standards of righteousness that God intends us to have. But through His mercy and grace, He provided a way for our sins to be forgiven through our acceptance of Christ Jesus—even though we don't deserve it. Coupled with grace (being given God's gift of forgiveness though we've done nothing to deserve it), mercy is shown because He loves us and only asks that we accept His Son by faith.[15]

God's love for mankind is so great that He bestows mercy and grace even to sinners. He provided a way for everyone to live in peace and to have the assurance of eternal salvation. However, all have fallen into sin, but God gives many chances and will show His love even when one rebels against Him. He is a merciful God. He shows compassion

---

[15] https://www.allaboutgod.com/god-of-mercy.htm

and forgiveness, and He shows grace, free and unmerited divine assistance or favor. In His mercy, He has made us alive with Christ, and by grace, we have been saved. This is found in Ephesians 2:4-5 and Titus 3:5-7. When alive in Christ, one will desire to learn, read, and understand the Bible and the mind of Christ.

> *But because of his great love for us, God, who is rich in mercy, made us alive with Christ even when we were dead in transgressions — it is by grace you have been saved.*
>
> *Ephesians 2:4-5*
> *New International Version (NIV)*

> *He saved us, not because of righteous things we had done, but because of his mercy. He saved us through the washing of rebirth and renewal by the Holy Spirit, whom he poured out on us generously through Jesus Christ our Savior, so that, having been justified by his grace, we might become heirs having the hope of eternal life.*
>
> *Titus 3:5-7*
> *New International Version (NIV)*

According to <u>Adventures in Mission</u> (myadventures.org), *"What does it mean to Live in Christ?"* explains:

> *Being alive in Christ and dead to the world means that the matters that consume so many people's lives with stress and anxiety are (or should be) of no concern to a Christian. We*

> *are concerned primarily with serving God, no matter what the cost. And that, in and of itself, is worth any pain or discomfort.[16]*

God is patient and forgives; therefore, He instructs us to forgive others in a loving and caring manner. Colossians 3:12 reveals that as Christians, we must show compassion, kindness, humility, gentleness, and patience towards one another. If one does not forgive, then God will not forgive, see Matthew 5:15. Even though someone may repent, one must be cautious by giving time for the offender to prove himself worthy of being trusted again. There are times when others will not ask for forgiveness, but we must forgive them anyway as we are not to hold on to grudges. Scriptures state that we should not only forgive but bless them, as stated in Matthew 6:15 and Matthew 5:43-44. In Hebrews 4:16, we are reminded that we can approach the throne of grace with confidence when we repent.

> *Therefore, as God's chosen people, holy and dearly loved, clothe yourselves with compassion, kindness, humility, gentleness and patience. Bear with each other and forgive one another if any of you has a grievance against someone. Forgive as the Lord forgave you.*
> *Colossians 3:12-13*
> *New International Version (NIV)*

---

[16] https://jeffgoins.myadventures.org/post/what-does-it-mean-to-be-alive-in-christ

> *But if you do not forgive others their sins, your Father will not forgive your sins.*
>
> *Matthew 6:15*
> *New International Version (NIV)*

> *Ye have heard that it hath been said, Thou shalt love thy neighbour, and hate thine enemy. But I say unto you, Love your enemies, bless them that curse you, do good to them that hate you, and pray for them which despitefully use you, and persecute you.*
>
> *Matthew 5:43-44*
> *King James Version (KJV)*

> *Let us then approach God's throne of grace with confidence, so that we may receive mercy and find grace to help us in our time of need.*
>
> *Hebrew 4:16*
> *New International Version (NIV)*

We must not take God's patience for granted because if we continue to reject Him, there will be a time that He will stop being merciful and not give any more chances, which will result in eternal death, see Luke 13:3.

> *I tell you, no! But unless you repent, you too will all perish.*
>
> *Luke 13:3*
> *New International Version (NIV)*

- God Calls Us to Repentance

Repentance as defined by the Cambridge dictionary:

> *The fact of <u>showing</u> that you are very <u>sorry</u> for something <u>bad</u> you have done in the past, and <u>wish</u> that you had not done it*[17]

Repentance as defined by Got Questions;

Question: "What is repentance, and is it necessary for salvation?"

> *Answer:* Many understand the term repentance to mean "a turning from sin." Regretting sin and turning from it is related to repentance, but it is not the precise meaning of the word. In the Bible, the word repent means "to change one's mind." The Bible also tells us that true repentance will result in a change of actions (Luke 3:8–14; Acts 3:19). In summarizing his ministry, Paul declares, "I preached that they should repent and turn to God and demonstrate their repentance by their deeds" (Acts 26:20). The full biblical definition of repentance is a change of mind that results in a change of action.[18]

---

[17] https://dictionary.cambridge.org/us/dictionary/english/repentance

[18] https://www.gotquestions.org/repentance.html

Produce fruit in keeping with repentance. And do not begin to say to yourselves, 'We have Abraham as our father.' For I tell you that out of these stones God can raise up children for Abraham. The ax is already at the root of the trees, and every tree that does not produce good fruit will be cut down and thrown into the fire." "What should we do then?" the crowd asked. John answered, "Anyone who has two shirts should share with the one who has none, and anyone who has food should do the same." Even tax collectors came to be baptized. "Teacher," they asked, "what should we do?" "Don't collect any more than you are required to," he told them. Then some soldiers asked him, "And what should we do?" He replied, "Don't extort money and don't accuse people falsely —be content with your pay."

Luke 3:8-14
New International Version (NIV)

Repent, then, and turn to God, so that your sins may be wiped out, that times of refreshing may come from the Lord

Acts 3:19
New International Version (NIV)

First to those in Damascus, then to those in Jerusalem and in all Judea, and then to the Gentiles, I preached that they should repent

> *and turn to God and demonstrate their repentance by their deeds.*
>
> *Acts 26:20*
> *New International Version (NIV)*

To establish a relationship, God will capture the heart of man to persuade him to turn to Him now and for eternity's sake. Romans 2:4 reminds us that He patiently waits, and His goodness is intended to lead us to repentance. While in this temporary home (earth), God's intention is for man to live harmonious with one another and to live a peaceful and abundant life. But Satan lies and wants to keep man in bondage because he is jealous since he rebelled against God and knows his fate. Ask a Christian parent what they hope for their children, and you will get the same answers. They want their children to be followers of Christ (Christian), be happy, loved, financially stable, talented, and much more. God is our Heavenly Father, and like a father, He has compassion on those that fear Him (Psalm 103:13), and He wants even more for His children. Daily, He desires to lead His children towards a righteous life. He wants them to love and be loved, filled with blessings enabling one to use them to proclaim the teachings of His word and to encourage one another. God does not want anyone to perish, and at the same time, He does not force anyone because He gives everyone a free will to choose the path one will take.

> *Or do you show contempt for the riches of his kindness, forbearance and patience, not*

> *realizing that God's kindness is intended to lead you to repentance?*
>
> *Romans 2:4*
> *New International Version (NIV)*

> *As a father has compassion on his children, so the Lord has compassion on those who fear him.*
>
> *Psalm 103:13*
> *New International Version (NIV)*

Repentance is necessary because apart from God's justice is eternal destruction as He judges sins. God is faithful as He judges both the righteous and the unrighteous. Psalm 75:7, Hebrews 10:30, Psalm 96:13, James 4, James 5, and Isaiah 33 reminds us that God is our judge.

> *It is God who judges: He brings one down, he exalts another.*
>
> *Psalm 75:7*
> *New International Version (NIV)*

> *For we know him who said, "It is mine to avenge; I will repay," and again, "The Lord will judge his people."*
>
> *Hebrews 10:30*
> *New International Version (NIV)*

> *Let all creation rejoice before the Lord, for he comes, he comes to judge the earth. He*

will judge the world in righteousness and the peoples in his faithfulness.

Psalm 96:13
New International Version (NIV)

There is only one Lawgiver and Judge, the one who is able to save and destroy.

James 4:12
New International Version (NIV)

Don't grumble against one another, brothers and sisters, or you will be judged. The Judge is standing at the door!

James 5:9
New International Version (NIV)

For the Lord is our judge, the Lord is our lawgiver, the Lord is our king; it is he who will save us.

Isaiah 33:22
New International Version (NIV

God will continue nudging us to repentance and to accept His teachings until we either receive Jesus Christ as our Savior and Lord and His righteous ways or sadly die without accepting Jesus and end up in misery due to the punishment inflicted while in Hell. In Matthew 25:41-46, Jesus describes hell as a place created for the punishment of the devil and his angels. But in Matthew 13:50, He further describes it as a place for wicked sinners inflicting the punishment of eternal fire, misery, and torment. Revelation

21:8, 2 Thessalonians 1:9, and Matthew 13:50 are other good sources about hell and eternal destruction.

> *"Then he will say to those on his left, 'Depart from me, you who are cursed, into the eternal fire prepared for the devil and his angels. For I was hungry and you gave me nothing to eat, I was thirsty and you gave me nothing to drink, I was a stranger and you did not invite me in, I needed clothes and you did not clothe me, I was sick and in prison and you did not look after me.'*
>
> *"They also will answer, 'Lord, when did we see you hungry or thirsty or a stranger or needing clothes or sick or in prison, and did not help you?'*
>
> *"He will reply, 'Truly I tell you, whatever you did not do for one of the least of these, you did not do for me.' "Then they will go away to eternal punishment, but the righteous to eternal life.*
>
> *Matthew 25:41-46*
> *New International Version (NIV)*

> *But the cowardly, the unbelieving, the vile, the murderers, the sexually immoral, those who practice magic arts, the idolaters and all liars —they will be consigned to the fiery lake of burning sulfur. This is the second death."*
>
> *Revelation 21:8*
> *New International Version (NIV)*

They will be punished with everlasting destruction and shut out from the presence of the Lord.

2 Thessalonians 1:9
New International Version (NIV)

And throw them into the blazing furnace, where there will be weeping and gnashing of teeth.

Matthew 13:50
New International Version (NIV)

- Eternal Salvation

Oxford Living Dictionary defines *eternity* as:

Theology: Endless life after death.[19]

Salvation, according to gotquestions.org, is described as:

What are we saved from? In the Christian doctrine of salvation, we are saved from "wrath," that is, from God's judgment of sin (Romans 5:9; 1 Thessalonians 5:9). Our sin has separated us from God, and the consequence of sin is death (Romans 6:23). Biblical salvation refers to our deliverance

---

[19] https://en.oxforddictionaries.com/definition/eternity

from the consequence of sin and therefore involves the removal of sin.[20]

Since we have now been justified by his blood, how much more shall we be saved from God's wrath through him!

Romans 5:9
New International Version (NIV)

For God did not appoint us to suffer wrath but to receive salvation through our Lord Jesus Christ.

1 Thessalonians 5:9
New International Version (NIV)

God's promise of eternal salvation comes through accepting Jesus Chris as personal Savior and Lord; this is found in the books of Amos 5:4, Psalms 37:39, Psalms 62:1-2, Acts 4:11-12, and John 10:28.

This is what the Lord says to Israel: "Seek me and live."

Amos 5:4
New International Version (NIV)

The salvation of the righteous comes from the Lord.

Psalms 37:39
New International Version (NIV)

---

[20] https://www.gotquestions.org/Christian-doctrine-salvation.html

> *Truly my soul finds rest in God; my salvation comes from him. Truly he is my rock and my salvation; he is my fortress, I will never be shaken.*
>
> *Psalms 62:1-2*
> *New International Version (NIV)*

> *Jesus is "'the stone you builders rejected, which has become the cornerstone.'*
>
> *Salvation is found in no one else, for there is no other name under heaven given to mankind by which we must be saved."*
>
> *Acts 4:11-12*
> *New International Version (NIV)*

> *(Jesus) I give them eternal life, and they shall never perish.*
>
> *John 10:28*
> *New International Version (NIV)*

To seek the Lord wholeheartedly, one must have faith in the risen Christ as the only way to enter the kingdom of God. In Hebrews 11:1 and Hebrews 11:6, we are reminded of the need for faith to have confidence and the assurance for what we do not see. Without faith, it is hard to please God since we have not seen Him, see John 6:46 and John 1:18. Salvation is a gift from God and cannot be bought or obtained by works, see Ephesians 2:8-9. In Romans 10:17, we are to read the Bible as we are reminded that the message of Jesus Christ is proclaimed through the Word of God, and faith comes from hearing the word. Several benefits of reading the word of God are: it gives instructions for living in righteousness, and it is necessary to stay in line with the will of God; it helps us discern right from wrong and to differentiate between Godly thinking and worldly thinking; the word is filled with God's many promises if we are obedient or not. If we remain in obedience to the word of God, some of the promises are peace, protection, forgiveness, encouragement, healing, power, wisdom, guidance, and to be an overcomer.

> *Now faith is confidence in what we hope for and assurance about what we do not see.*
> *Hebrews 11:1*
> *New International Version (NIV)*

> *And without faith it is impossible to please God, because anyone who comes to him must believe that he exists and that he rewards those who earnestly seek him.*
> *Hebrews 11:6*
> *New International Version (NIV)*

> *No one has seen the Father except the one who is from God; only he has seen the Father.*
> *John 6:46*
> *New International Version (NIV)*

> *No one has ever seen God, but the one and only Son, who is himself God and is in closest relationship with the Father, has made him known.*
> *John 1:18*
> *New International Version (NIV)*

> *For it is by grace you have been saved, through faith —and this is not from yourselves, it is the gift of God. not by works—so that no one can boast.*
>
> *Ephesians 2:8-9*
> *New International Version (NIV)*

> *Consequently, faith comes from hearing the message, and the message is heard through the word about Christ.*
>
> *Romans 10:17*
> *New International Version (NIV)*

Eternal salvation refers to physical death from earthly life to our new home in heaven for those that accept Jesus as their Savior. The English Oxford Dictionaries define Heaven as:

> *Theology - A state of being eternally in the presence of God after death.*
> *'the everlasting happiness with God that we call heaven*[21]

In Acts 1:11, the Bible tells us that when Jesus was taken into heaven, the "Men of Galilee" were looking into the sky for the return of Jesus, as He had promised that He would return for them. The promise extends to His return and taking His children with Him to a New Heaven and a New Earth. In John 14:1-3, Jesus promises to go and prepare a place for his children, and He states there are many rooms (King James Version uses the word mansion). In Isaiah

---

[21] https://en.oxforddictionaries.com/definition/heaven

35:5-6, there will not be any blind, deaf, lame, or mute person in heaven. In Revelations 21:21, Revelation 21:1-4, and Isaiah 65:17, we are given a description of heaven: paradise with no more tears and pain, no more death and no more mourning, and streets paved with gold.

> *"Men of Galilee," they said, "why do you stand here looking into the sky? This same Jesus, who has been taken from you into heaven, will come back in the same way you have seen him go into heaven."*
>
> *Acts 1:11*
> *New International Version (NIV)*

> *Do not let your hearts be troubled. You believe in God; believe also in me. My Father's house has many rooms; if that were not so, would I have told you that I am going there to prepare a place for you? And if I go and prepare a place for you, I will come back and take you to be with me that you also may be where I am.*
>
> *John 14:1-3*
> *New International Version (NIV)*

> *In my Father's house are many mansions.*
>
> *John 14:2*
> *King James Version (KJV)*

> *Then will the eyes of the blind be opened and the ears of the deaf unstopped.*

Then will the lame leap like a deer, and the mute tongue shout for joy.

Isaiah 35:5-6
New International Version (NIV)

The twelve gates were twelve pearls, each gate made of a single pearl. The great street of the city was of gold, as pure as transparent glass.

Revelations 21:21
New International Version (NIV)

New Heavens and a New Earth

Then I saw "a new heaven and a new earth," for the first heaven and the first earth had passed away, and there was no longer any sea. I saw the Holy City, the new Jerusalem, coming down out of heaven from God, prepared as a bride beautifully dressed for her husband. And I heard a loud voice from the throne saying, "Look! God's dwelling place is now among the people, and he will dwell with them. They will be his people, and God himself will be with them and be their God. 'He will wipe every tear from their eyes. There will be no more death' or mourning or crying or pain, for the old order of things has passed away."

Revelations 21:1-4
New International Version (NIV)

New Heavens and a New Earth

"See, I will create new heavens and a new earth. The former things will not be remembered, nor will they come to mind. But be glad and rejoice forever in what I will create, for I will create Jerusalem to be a delight and its people a joy. I will rejoice over Jerusalem and take delight in my people; the sound of weeping and of crying will be heard in it no more.

Isaiah 65:17
New International Version (NIV)

- God Will Never Forsake Us

Hebrews 13:5, Jeremiah 29:13, Deuteronomy 4:29-31, Psalm 40:16, and John 14:18 reveal a merciful God who will not abandon us nor leave us like orphans if we wholeheartedly seek Him and turn from our wicked way. With so much corruption abroad and in our backyards, God will still have mercy on us and will not turn His back when we repent and turn from a sinful lifestyle, see 2 Chronicles 7:14.

> *God has said, "Never will I leave you; never will I forsake you."*
>
> *Hebrews 13:5*
> *New International Version (NIV)*

> *You will seek me and find me when you seek me with all your heart.*
>
> *Jeremiah 29:13*
> *New International Version (NIV)*

A Call from God

But if from there you seek the Lord your God, you will find him if you seek him with all your heart and with all your soul. When you are in distress and all these things have happened to you, then in later days you will return to the Lord your God and obey him. For the Lord your God is a merciful God; he will not abandon or destroy you or forget the covenant with your ancestors, which he confirmed to them by oath.

Deuteronomy 4: 29-31
New International Version (NIV)

But may all who seek you rejoice and be glad in you; may those who long for your saving help always say, "The Lord is great!"

Psalm 40:16
New International Version (NIV)

I will not leave you as orphans.

John 14:18
New International Version (NIV)

If my people, who are called by my name, will humble themselves and pray and seek my face and turn from their wicked ways, then I will hear from heaven, and I will forgive their sin and will heal their land.

2 Chronicles 7:14
New International Version (NIV)

In Romans 8:15, Mark 14:36, and Galatians 4:6, we have a Father we can call "Abba Father" (An intimate term like daddy). This is possible because we can have a personal relationship like that of a parent; thus, we can call upon Him at any time. Often parents may find themselves too busy, and when a child approaches them with a question, the child may get the response of, "not now, I am too busy." Be assured our communication with God is always open, and He is never too busy for us. He cares for the small things in life, even a parking space near the front door and the more pressing issue of life.

> *The Spirit you received does not make you slaves, so that you live in fear again; rather, the Spirit you received brought about your adoption to sonship. And by him we cry, "Abba, Father."*
>
> *Romans 8:15*
> *New International Version (NIV)*

> *Going a little farther, he fell to the ground and prayed that if possible the hour might pass from him. "Abba, Father," he said, "everything is possible for you. Take this cup from me. Yet not what I will, but what you will."*
>
> *Mark 14:35-36*
> *New International Version (NIV)*

> *Because you are his sons, God sent the Spirit of his Son into our hearts, the Spirit who calls out, "Abba, Father." So you are no longer a*

slave, but God's child; and since you are his child, God has made you also an heir.

Galatians 4:5-6
New International Version (NIV)

Got Questions defines Abba Father as follows:

Question: "What does it mean that God is our Abba Father?"

Answer: In Scripture there are many different names used to describe God. While all the names of God are important in many ways, the name "Abba Father" is one of the most significant names of God in understanding how He relates to people. The word Abba is an Aramaic word that means "Father." It was a common term that expressed affection and confidence and trust. Abba signifies the close, intimate relationship of a father and his child, as well as the childlike trust that a young child puts in his "daddy."[22]

---

[22] https://www.gotquestions.org/Abba-Father.html

CHAPTER 4

Free Will

Merriam Webster defines free will as:

> *Definition of free will*
>
> *1: voluntary choice or decision - I do this of my own free will*
>
> *2: freedom of humans to make choices that are not determined by prior causes or by divine intervention.*[23]

From the beginning of creation, God created man with the ability to make choices; He gave man free will. Free will allow man to choose either obedience that leads to eternal salvation or disobedience that leads to eternal damnation. The Word tells us that everyone must make a choice to choose the Lord or worldly ways, as stated in Joshua 24:15. Free will was demonstrated in the Garden of Eden when God gave Adam and Eve the ability to follow His

---

[23] https://www.merriam-webster.com/dictionary/freewill

instruction not to eat from the forbidden tree of knowledge of good and evil, as found in Genesis 2:17.

> *And if it is evil in your eyes to serve the Lord, choose this day whom you will serve, whether the gods your fathers served in the region beyond the River, or the gods of the Amorites in whose land you dwell. But as for me and my house, we will serve the Lord."*
>
> *Joshua 24:15*
> *English Standard Version (ESV)*

> *But you must not eat from the tree of the knowledge of good and evil, for when you eat from it you will certainly die."*
>
> *Genesis 2:17*
> *New International Version (NIV)*

When God created the heavens and earth, He was pleased and found that everything He made was perfect, Genesis 1:31. From the dust of the ground, God formed Adam and breathed into his nostrils the breath of life, Genesis 2:7, and God created man in His own image, Genesis 1:27.

> *God saw all that he had made, and it was very good.*
>
> *Genesis 1:31*
> *New International Version (NIV)*

> *Then the Lord God formed a man from the dust of the ground and breathed into*

> *his nostrils the breath of life, and the man became a living being.*
>
> *Genesis 2:7*
> *New International Version (NIV)*

> *So God created mankind in his own image, in the image of God he created them; male and female he created them.*
>
> *Genesis 1:27*
> *New International Version (NIV)*

When God created the universe and everything in it, He did not find a suitable helper for Adam and because He had companion for Adam, out of Adam's rib He made the woman, Genesis 2:20b-22:

> *But for Adam no suitable helper was found. So the Lord God caused the man to fall into a deep sleep; and while he was sleeping, he took one of the man's ribs and then closed up the place with flesh. Then the Lord God made a woman from the rib he had taken out of the man, and he brought her to the man.*
>
> *Genesis 2:20b-22*
> *New International Version (NIV)*

God did not want puppets or robots, so He created man in His own image with the ability to make decisions; therefore, we have a free will to choose between good or evil and to choose between accepting Jesus as our Savior and Lord or denying Him. The fall resulted from man listening to Satan's lies and falling into his trap by being disobedient to God. Everyone is responsible for his own choice to accept Jesus and become a part of the family of God, thus being sons and daughters. Here are several verses in the Bible that refer to Christians as His children: 2 Corinthians 6:18, Galatians 4:6-7, Galatians 3:26, Romans 8:14-16, Revelation 21:7, and John 1:12. In Ezekiel 18:30-32, since God gives everyone a free will, God pleaded with the Israelites to make a choice to repent and not die. God will not force anyone as this would go against His laws and take away our free will.

> *And I will be a father to you, and you shall be sons and daughters to me, says the Lord Almighty.*
>
> *2 Corinthians 6:18*
> *English Standard Version (ESV)*

> *And because you are sons, God has sent the Spirit of his Son into our hearts, crying, "Abba! Father!" So you are no longer a slave, but a son, and if a son, then an heir through God.*
>
> *Galatians 4:6-7*
> *English Standard Version (ESV)*

> *For in Christ Jesus you are all sons of God, through faith.*
>
> *Galatians 3:26*
> *English Standard Version (ESV)*

> *For all who are led by the Spirit of God are sons of God. For you did not receive the spirit*

of slavery to fall back into fear, but you have received the Spirit of adoption as sons, by whom we cry, "Abba! Father!"

Romans 8:14-16
English Standard Version (ESV)

The one who conquers will have this heritage, and I will be his God and he will be my son.
Revelations 21:7
English Standard Version (ESV)

But to all who did receive him, who believed in his name, he gave the right to become children of God, who were born, not of blood nor of the will of the flesh nor of the will of man, but of God.

John 1:12
English Standard Version (ESV)

"Therefore, you Israelites, I will judge each of you according to your own ways, declares the Sovereign Lord. Repent! Turn away from all your offenses; then sin will not be your downfall. Rid yourselves of all the offenses you have committed, and get a new heart and a new spirit. Why will you die, people of Israel? For I take no pleasure in the death of anyone, declares the Sovereign Lord. Repent and live!
Ezekiel 18:30-32
New International Version (NIV)

We will not get into heaven on our own merits or works performed by us or those performed by our family or friends. We are to verbally accept Christ and make a personal commitment to turn from worldly living towards righteous living by following the directions we find in the scriptures. The following verses, Romans 10:9 and John 3:16, give instructions regarding accepting Christ as our Personal Savior.

> *If you declare with your mouth, "Jesus is Lord," and believe in your heart that God raised him from the dead, you will be saved. For it is with your heart that you believe and are justified, and it is with your mouth that you profess your faith and are saved.*
>
> *Romans 10:9*
> *New International Version (NIV)*

> *For God so loved the world that he gave his one and only Son, that whoever believes in him shall not perish but have eternal life.*
>
> *John 3:16*
> *New International Version (NIV)*

Deciding to accept Jesus Christ means daily living in faith by trusting Him. Faith comes by believing in something we cannot see, and believing comes from hearing the Word. Romans 10:17, 1 Thessalonians 2:13, John 4:42, and John 20:31 are a reminder of the importance of reading the Bible because it is a tool for learning about God the Father, Jesus the Son of God, and the Holy Spirit. This affirms that the Word is from God for encouragement and the promise of protection and prosperity. Additionally, Jeremiah 29:11 reminds us that the Lord has a plan to prosper and not harm us with the hope of the future. By reading the Bible, we learn what the will of God is for our lives as God speaks to us through His word. He gives us spiritual gifts to build the Kingdom of God, such as wisdom, faith, healing, and prophecy; see 1 Corinthians 12:8-11 for the entire list. It does not specify regarding decisions we must make for our lives, such as should we marry and/or who we should marry, or perhaps what career or job to take, but it gives us the principles to live by, which, in turn, helps us make these decisions. Reading the word of God will give an understanding of His wisdom and His heart desires. As our body needs daily nourishment, we need spiritual nourishment for faith and to learn and affirm sound doctrine to understand righteous living from ungodly living. Be vigilant so that you can grasp the meaning and not be fooled by unbelievers or false teachings and thus be equipped to teach others so they too can hear what the Lord says 2 Timothy 3:16. While we read the Bible, we are still, and as we meditate on his teachings, our spirit is calmed, which helps us relax and not be anxious, which benefits our health.

> *Consequently, faith comes from hearing the message, and the message is heard through the word about Christ.*
>
> *Romans 10:17*
> *New International Version (NIV)*

And we also thank God continually because, when you received the word of God, which you heard from us, you accepted it not as a human word, but as it actually is, the word of God, which is indeed at work in you who believe.

1 Thessalonians 2:13
New International Version (NIV)

They said to the woman, "We no longer believe just because of what you said; now we have heard for ourselves, and we know that this man really is the Savior of the world."

John 4:42
New International Version (NIV)

But these are written that you may believe that Jesus is the Messiah, the Son of God, and that by believing you may have life in his name.

John 20:31
New International Version (NIV)

For I know the plans I have for you," declares the Lord, "plans to prosper you and not to harm you, plans to give you hope and a future.
Jeremiah 29:11
New International Version (NIV)

To one there is given through the Spirit a message of wisdom, to another a message of

> *knowledge by means of the same Spirit, to another faith by the same Spirit, to another gifts of healing by that one Spirit, to another miraculous powers, to another prophecy, to another distinguishing between spirits, to another speaking in different kinds of tongues, and to still another the interpretation of tongues. All these are the work of one and the same Spirit, and he distributes them to each one, just as he determines.*
>
> *1 Corinthians 12:8-11*
> *New International Version (NIV)*

> *All Scripture is God-breathed and is useful for teaching, rebuking, correcting and training in righteousness, so that the servant of God may be thoroughly equipped for every good work.*
>
> *2 Timothy 3:16:17*
> *New International Version (NIV)*

Choosing to follow God means we believe that He created the universe by His word as He commanded, and not out of visible things; this is found in Hebrews 11:1-3. We believe that Jesus died and arose as a final payment for our sins, as stated in Galatians 3:13-14. Other verses to back up the fact that Jesus paid the final payment for our sins are found in 1 Peter 1:18-19, 1 Peter 2:24, and Romans 5:8.

> *Now faith is confidence in what we hope for and assurance about what we do not see. This is what the ancients were commended for. By*

faith we understand that the universe was formed at God's command, so that what is seen was not made out of what was visible.

Hebrews 11:1-3
New International Version (NIV)

But the law is not of faith, rather "The one who does them shall live by them." Christ redeemed us from the curse of the law by becoming a curse for us—for it is written, "Cursed is everyone who is hanged on a tree"— so that in Christ Jesus the blessing of Abraham might come to the Gentiles, so that we might receive the promised Spirit through faith.

Galatians 3:13-14
English Standard Version (ESV)

Knowing that you were ransomed from the futile ways inherited from your forefathers, not with perishable things such as silver or gold, but with the precious blood of Christ, like that of a lamb without blemish or spot.

1 Peter 1:18-19
English Standard Version (ESV)

He himself bore our sins in his body on the tree, that we might die to sin and live to righteousness. By his wounds you have been healed.

1 Peter 2:24
English Standard Version (ESV)

> *But God shows his love for us in that while we*
> *were still sinners, Christ died for us.*
> *Romans 5:8*
> *English Standard Version (ESV)*

Since we are all born into a sinful world and do not have the means nor can we buy our way into heaven, God's mercy was demonstrated to us when Jesus paid the price by enduring and dying a crucial death on the cross. He was mocked, spit upon, flogged, crucified, and three days later, He arose so we could have healing and the assurance of eternal salvation. Jesus was the Sinless One who died for us, even though we did not deserve it; that is why it is recorded in Romans 6:23 the wages of sin is death, but the gift of eternal life is found by accepting Jesus Christ as our Savior.

> *For the wages of sin is death, but the free gift*
> *of God is eternal life in Christ Jesus our Lord.*
> *Romans 6:23*
> *English Standard Version (ESV)*

God knew the only way to escape from the curse of God's law and to be free was for someone to pay the penalty once and for all for our sins. Therefore, as Christian, our acceptance of Jesus must be accompanied by a total commitment to surrender our will and strive to live a righteous life. We are to be servants of God by caring for one another, visiting the sick and those in prisons, helping the helpless, and feeding the hungry. We should have a total commitment to worshiping, praising, singing, loving Him, and loving our brother and sisters in Christ to His glory. We do this by choosing His will and not our own. When we make the choice to accept Jesus and follow his way, our love for God must be above all others. When my son was a young boy, I used to tell him, "Son, as you know, I love you with all my heart, but we must love God even more than anyone." A close relationship with God will enable us to hear his voice often through the reading of the word, our thoughts, when the gospel is preached, or in conversation with other Christians. In the book of John 10:27-28, God calls us His sheep as He is our Shepherd who cares for us, and He promises never to forsake us.

> *My sheep hear my voice, and I know them, and they follow me. I give them eternal life, and they will never perish, and no one will snatch them out of my hand.*
>
> *John 10:27-28*
> *English Standard Version (ESV)*

God, our loving Shepherd, watches and protects us like His sheep; but unlike a sheep, we have a free will to choose to commit to the ways of the Lord or not. In Deuteronomy 30:19-20, we are instructed to choose life and to obey His voice. When making choices, we must be aware of the consequences or benefits, knowing that what we sow, we will reap. I've heard others say, "What goes around comes around." However, you will be treated the way you treat others. Luke 6:38 and Mark 4:24-25 reminds us to be cautious to whatever measure is used for either blessings or curses, as it will come back like a boomerang. In 2Corinthians 9:6, if one sows sparingly, one will reap sparingly, or if one sows generously, one will reap generously. In Galatians 6:7-

8, we are instructed that we will reap what we sow, that is, if we sow from the flesh, we will reap destruction, but if we sow to please the Spirit of God, we will reap eternal life. The concept of the reflections of water echoes the idea of what you sow; you will reap. If you look into a body of water as you extend your hand and pretend to take from it, your reflection will take from you. If you pretend to give or to throw something in, your reflection will give back to you. If you only take from others, what you have will eventually be taken from you. If you give generously, you will receive generously.

> *I call heaven and earth to witness against you today, that I have set before you life and death, blessing and curse. Therefore choose life, that you and your offspring may live, loving the Lord your God, obeying his voice and holding fast to him, for he is your life and length of days, that you may dwell in the land that the Lord swore to your fathers, to Abraham, to Isaac, and to Jacob, to give them."*
>
> *Deuteronomy 30:19-20*
> *English Standard Version (ESV)*

> *Give, and it will be given to you. A good measure, pressed down, shaken together and running over, will be poured into your lap. For with the measure you use, it will be measured to you."*
>
> *Luke 6:38*
> *New International Version (NIV)*

Consider carefully what you hear," he continued. "With the measure you use, it will be measured to you—and even more. Whoever has will be given more; whoever does not have, even what they have will be taken from them."

Mark 4:24-25
New International Version (NIV)

Remember this: Whoever sows sparingly will also reap sparingly, and whoever sows generously will also reap generously. Each of you should give what you have decided in your heart to give, not reluctantly or under compulsion, for God loves a cheerful giver.

2 Corinthians 9:6-7
New International Version (NIV)

Do not be deceived: God cannot be mocked. A man reaps what he sows. Whoever sows to please their flesh, from the flesh will reap destruction; whoever sows to please the Spirit, from the Spirit will reap eternal life.

Galatians 6:7-8
New International Version (NIV)

While God has given us the free will to choose to either live a righteous life or live a sinful life, He has also provided a way for us to step away from temptation, as stated in 1Corinthians 10:13. In Colossians 1:1-14, God provides a way for us to be an overcomer, that is to face sinful problems, walk away from the worldly living, and block the darts the devil throws our way. This is done through the power of God when we put our trust and faith in Him. In Ephesians 6:10-18, we are given the weapons to use in this spiritual battle; it is referred to as the "Armor of God."

The belt of truth is the truths found by reading the Bible; the breastplate of righteousness, choosing to live in righteousness versus living a worldly life; the shoes of the gospel of peace, spread the good news to everyone; the shield of faith, believing in the Living God as Jesus Christ is the only mediator to the Father; the helmet of salvation, having the assurance of eternal salvation in Jesus' name; and the sword of the Spirit, which is the word of God.

> *No temptation has overtaken you that is not common to man. God is faithful, and he will not let you be tempted beyond your ability, but with the temptation he will also provide the way of escape, that you may be able to endure it.*
>
> *1 Corinthians 10:13*
> *English Standard Version (ESV)*

> *For he has rescued us from the dominion of darkness and brought us into the kingdom of the Son he loves, in whom we have redemption, the forgiveness of sins.*
>
> *Colossians 1:13-14*
> *New International Version (NIV)*

Finally, be strong in the Lord and in his mighty power. Put on the full armor of God, so that you can take your stand against the devil's schemes. For our struggle is not against flesh and blood, but against the rulers, against the authorities, against the powers of this dark world and against the spiritual forces of evil in the heavenly realms. Therefore, put on the full armor of God, so that when the day of evil comes, you may be able to stand your ground, and after you have done everything, to stand. Stand firm then, with the belt of truth buckled around your waist, with the breastplate of righteousness in place, and with your feet fitted with the readiness that comes from the gospel of peace. In addition to all this, take up the shield of faith, with which you can extinguish all the flaming arrows of the evil one. Take the helmet of salvation and the sword of the Spirit, which is the word of God. And pray in the Spirit on all occasions with all kinds of prayers and requests. With this in mind, be alert and always keep on praying for all the Lord's people.
Ephesians 6:10-18
New International Version (NIV)

Humankind can be exasperating at times. One minute, we are praising God, and then in the next minute, we find ourselves complaining and not trusting in God. This allows us to exercise our free will, so that not only in the good times we praise and thank God but also when facing obstacles in life. That is a time when we especially need to trust in our loving God. When unwanted circumstances infringe our comfort zone, it is often a time of growth. We must learn to have patience just as God is patient with us and wait upon the Lord, knowing that His timing is perfect Psalm 27:14. Keep in mind that God is love (1John 4:16 and 1John 4:8); love is patient (1 Corinthians 13:4), and He is patient toward everyone as He does not want anyone to perish as stated in 2Peter 3:9.

> *Wait for the Lord; be strong and take heart and wait for the Lord.*
> *Psalm 27:14*
> *New International Version (NIV)*

> *God is love. Whoever lives in love lives in God, and God in them.*
> *1 John 4:16*
> *New International Version (NIV)*

> *Whoever does not love does not know God, because God is love.*
> *1 John 4:8*
> *New International Version (NIV*

> *Love is patient, love is kind.*
> *1 Corinthians 13:4*
> *New International Version (NIV)*

The Lord is not slow to fulfill his promise as some count slowness, but is patient toward you, not wishing that any should perish, but that all should reach repentance.

2 Peter 3:9
English Standard Version (ESV)

CHAPTER

5

Instinct for God

As a child, I instinctually knew how to pray for the protection of my loved ones whenever I felt they were in danger. In a study performed at the University of Oxford, it was resolved that it is in human nature for people to instinctually believe in gods and the afterlife.

> A three-year international research project, directed by two academics at the University of Oxford, finds that humans have natural tendencies to believe in gods and the afterlife.
>
> The researchers point out that the project was not setting out to prove the existence of god or otherwise, but sought to find out whether concepts such as gods and an afterlife appear to be entirely taught or basic expressions of human nature.[24]

---

[24] https://www.sciencedaily.com/releases/2011/07/110714103828.htm

Romans 1:19-20 reminds us that since God has made it clear by His invisible qualities, we do not have an excuse to deny His existence.

> *Since what may be known about God is plain to them, because God has made it plain to them. For since the creation of the world God's invisible qualities—his eternal power and divine nature—have been clearly seen, being understood from what has been made, so that people are without excuse.*
> *Romans 1:19-20*
> *New International Version (NIV)*

The evidence that God exists can be seen all around us. He created the planets, and He sustains them. Just look at the wonders of the world or look towards the universe for its majestic beauty and the placement of the universe to know this to be true. In Psalm 104:24-25, Psalm 8:3-4, and Psalm 19:1-6, we read about the wisdom, testimony, revelation, power, and majesty of God's creation.

> *How many are your works, Lord! In wisdom you made them all; the earth is full of your creatures. There is the sea, vast and spacious, teeming with creatures beyond number—living things both large and small.*
> *Psalm 104:24-25*
> *New International Version (NIV)*

> *When I consider Your heavens, the work of your fingers, the moon and the stars, which*

you have set in place, what is mankind that you are mindful of them, human beings that you care for them?

Psalm 8: 3-4
New International Version (NIV)

The heavens declare the glory of God; the skies proclaim the work of his hands.

Day after day they pour forth speech; night after night they reveal knowledge.

They have no speech, they use no words; no sound is heard from them. Yet their voice goes out into all the earth, their words to the ends of the world. In the heavens God has pitched a tent for the sun. It is like a bridegroom coming out of his chamber, like a champion rejoicing to run his course. It rises at one end of the heavens and makes its circuit to the other; nothing is deprived of its warmth.

Psalm 19:1-6
New International Version (NIV)

Our natural tendencies or consciousness brings out our curiosity assimilating thoughts within our heart and mind. Our curiosity to seek God comes because God seeks out His children to know Him through Jesus Christ. Sometimes we think or wonder just how it is possible for the universe to exist. As we look in every direction, it is possible to see the intricacy of God's creation, yet understanding how it works is complex and, at times, unfathomable. Here are some examples of what we see but do not have the real grasp of how it works, except that we know it is possible by the hand of God.

- We can see that the Solar System, Mercury, Venus, Earth, Mars, Jupiter, Saturn, Uranus, Neptune, and Pluto, also referred to as a dwarf planet, stay suspended in space by gravitational forces. Let's look at the Moon that orbits the Earth once every 27.322 days, as stated by space.com in the article *"Does the Moon Rotate?"*

> The moon orbits the Earth once every 27.322 days. It also takes approximately 27 days for the moon to rotate once on its axis. As a result, the moon does not seem to be spinning but appears to observers from Earth to remain almost perfectly still. Nov 14, 2017[25]

The moon is suspended in space, and scientifically, we can explain why this occurs. *Ask an Astronomer* explains:

> A simple answer to "why does the Moon stay suspended in the air?" is this: There is a gravitational force between the Moon and the Earth that tries to pull the Moon toward the latter. This constant tug on the Moon as it moves around the Earth is called

---

[25] https://www.space.com/24871-does-the-moon-rotate.html

a "centripetal" force. The "centrifugal" force balances this force that pulls on the Earth and keeps the moon in motion. It is the balance between the centripetal and centrifugal forces that keep the Moon in orbit around the Earth.

One can be more persistent than that, however, and this is where the subtlety comes about. Why do the centripetal and centrifugal forces exactly balance each other? Because otherwise, the Moon would come crashing into Earth. But why does the Moon not come crashing into Earth? Because the centrifugal force exactly balances the centripetal force. The reasoning here is circular: the simple explanation above provides a way of understanding how the Moon stays in orbit around the Earth, but not precisely why. Einstein, in the early 1900s only supplied the why.

A more thorough answer to "Why does the Moon stay suspended in the air?" is the following. We think that Einstein's Theory of General Relativity explains the properties of space and time in the Universe. Within that theory, objects with mass curve spacetime in their vicinity, and this curvature influences the motions of other objects. The greater the mass and density of the object, the larger the curvature of spacetime that results. So, the Moon orbits the Earth because the Earth curves spacetime in the vicinity of the Moon. Though the Moon itself curves space as well (since it has mass), the curvature in the vicinity of the Moon is dominated by the Earth, which "tells" the Moon to orbit the Earth, given the Moon's current position and motion in the sky. It is this interplay between mass and curvature that causes the gravitational and the centripetal forces in the first place, and thus why the simple explanation holds.

The difference between the two answers is very subtle, but it boils down to this:

First case: - Why does the Moon orbit the Earth? It just does. And you can understand how it does by analyzing the forces on the Moon caused by its orbit and finding the forces pushing in and out are equal.

Second case: - Why does the Moon orbit the Earth? Because the Earth distorts spacetime in the vicinity of the Moon and causes it to orbit the Earth the way it does and the balance of forces to come out the way it does. This page was last updated on July 18, 2015.[26]

Okay, but doesn't this leave you with the question of how it is possible; who controls all of these forces? God set this in motion from the beginning of time through His creation. So how can anyone question the existence of God? I have heard people say there has to be a higher power, yes, and it is God, our Creator.

- My favorite flower is the Cattleya Orchid, sometimes referred to as the Queen of Orchids, and it is often used in corsages. These beautiful plants are sold at a high price, especially in the international market. They come in a wide range of colors and have the largest flowers in the Orchid family. Orchids come in different sizes, shapes, colors, scent, and they can last anywhere from a few months to 6 months; and I have heard that there are about 53 species and thousands of hybrids. A couple of flowers that I find interesting are the ones that resemble a monkey (Monkey Orchid) and an owl (Owl Orchid). Some of these flowering Orchid plants display a unique formation and intricate design resembling bees or insects. The resemblance of the

---

[26] http://curious.astro.cornell.edu/about-us/44-our-solar-system/the-moon/general-questions/109-how-does-the-moon-stay-suspended-in-the-air-intermediate

flowers to insects or bees is so perfect that it has been said that the insects are fooled. Pollination occurs when male bees try to mate with the flower resembling female bees as their appearance, and enticing smell can fool them. With such precision and intricacy of the Orchid's formation, the flower's beauty can confirm that they are created by God.

- Consider the Bald Eagle, our national bird which is unique to North America. It is a bird of prey, a sea eagle that will eat fish, the food they mooch off other birds, or stolen food. They build their enormous nest high on the top of tall trees, which they use for perching, roosting, and nesting. The trees must be located near large bodies of water like seacoast and lakes with good visibility to their prey. Their feet, legs, and beak are yellow; their back and breast are blackish-brown; their head, neck, and tail are white, and their eyes are pale yellow. The following information about eagles were taken from ThoughtCo.com:

Males and females look the same, but mature females are about 25% larger than males. An adult eagle's body length ranges from 70 to 102 cm (28 to 40 in), with a wingspan of

> *1.8 to 2.3 m (5.9 to 7.5 ft) and a mass of 3 to 6 kg (6.6 to 13.9 lbs.).*[27]
>
> *Bald eagles truly have eagle-eye vision. Their vision is sharper than <u>any human's</u>, and their field of view is wider. In addition, eagles can see <u>ultraviolet light</u>. Like cats, the birds have an inner eyelid called a nictitating membrane. Eagles can close their main eyelids, yet still see through the translucent protective membrane.*[28]

They soar with their wings almost flat, According to *Bald Eagle Information Description Page 2:*

> To help them soar, eagles use thermals, which are rising currents of warm air and up-drafts generated by terrains such as valley edges or mountain slopes. Soaring is accomplished with very little wing-flapping, enabling them to conserve energy. Long-distance migration flights are accomplished by climbing high in a thermal, then gliding downward to catch the next thermal where the process is repeated. Several eagles soaring in a thermal together are described as a "kettle of eagles." (Courtesy of Marybeth Garrigan) Bald eagles can fly to an altitude

---

[27] https://www.thoughtco.com/bald-eagle-facts-4174386
[28] https://www.thoughtco.com/bald-eagle-facts-4174386

of 10,000 feet. During level flight, a bald eagle can achieve speeds of about 30 to 35 mph. An eagle's wings are long and broad, making them effective for soaring. To help reduce turbulence as air passes over the end of the wing, the tips of the feathers at the end of the wings are tapered so that when the eagle fully extends its wings, the tips are widely separated.[29]

Wow, these birds are amazing and a beautiful sight to see when they are soaring across the sky. Yes, there is a God, and this is one of His creations to prove it.

- What about an airplane? I have had opportunities to travel, and I am amazed at the size and weight of an international plane. They hold approximately 500 people plus food, luggage, and fuel, not to mention the weight of the plane, which is substantially more weight than an average plane.

  A 747-400 plane at takeoff can weigh approximately 910,000 pounds depending on the style of the plane.[30]

---

[29] http://www.baldeagleinfo.com/eagle/eagle8.html
[30] http://www.flugzeuginfo.net/acdata_php/acdata_7474_en.php

While an average plane like a Boeing 737-800 can fly with the average weight at takeoff being 172,500 pounds.[31]

How is it possible for a plane to fly when it is so big and heavy?

According to *NASA, How Do Planes Fly? How do airplanes stay in the air?*

- Lift pushes the airplane up. The way air moves around the wings give the airplane lift. The shape of the wings helps with lift, too.
- Weight is the force that pulls the airplane toward Earth. Airplanes are built so that their weight is spread from front to back. This keeps the airplane balanced.
- Thrust is the force that moves the airplane forward. Engines give thrust to airplanes. Sometimes an engine turns a propeller. Sometimes it is a jet engine. It doesn't matter as long as air keeps going over the wings.
- Drag slows the airplane. You can feel drag when you walk against a strong wind. Airplanes are designed to let air pass around them with less drag.

---

[31] http://www.flugzeuginfo.net/acdata_php/acdata_7378_en.php

- An airplane flies when all four forces work together. But, most airplanes need one more thing: They need a pilot to fly them![32]

God's infinite wisdom has provided a way for this to be possible; that such a massive plane can fly across the flawless sky.

> God created water on the first day of creation (Genesis 1:1), and on the second day, God separated the water from the sky. God was setting the earth so that plants could grow and all living creatures could survive since water would be a necessity. (Genesis 1:6-8).

> *In the beginning God created the heavens and the earth. Now the earth was formless and empty, darkness was over the surface of the deep, and the Spirit of God was hovering over the waters.*
>
> *Genesis 1:1*
> *New International Version (NIV)*

> *And God said, "Let there be a vault between the waters to separate water from water." So God made the vault and separated the water under the vault from the water above it. And it was so. God called the vault "sky." And*

---

[32] https://www.nasa.gov/audience/forstudents/k-4/stories/ames-how-do-planes-fly-text.html

*there was evening, and there was morning —
the second day.*

Genesis 1:6-8
New International Version (NIV)

No living creature, whether animal or human can survive without water as it only a matter of a few days before one dies without it. Our bodies need water as it plays an important part in the process of our bodies' functions. Therefore, health experts will recommend eating foods that contain fluids and drinking water daily, as this can affect one's energy level and brain function. We need to replenish water in order not to get dehydrated. Water helps regulate the body's temperature and maintain all body functions. Water is made up of two compounds hydrogen and oxygen (H_2O); it is nearly colorless, odorless, and tasteless. The temperature of water changes depending on the location, and it can range from freezing temperatures to extremely burning heat.

According to Quora in the article

What is the number of a normal temperature of water?

> *Room temperature of water is 20-25-degree Celsius, Freezing point 0 Celsius, and Boiling point 100 Celsius.*[33]

---

[33] https://www.quora.com/What-is-the-number-of-a-normal-temperature-of-water

"Water" Written By Steven S. Zumdahl Last Updated was Jan 3, 2019. Ice as it reacts in an unusual way than most chemical entities:

> Although the sight of cubes floating in a glass of ice water is commonplace, such behavior is unusual for chemical entities. For almost every other compound, the state is denser than the liquid state; thus, the solid would sink to the bottom of the liquid. The fact that ice floats on water are exceedingly important in the natural world because the ice that forms on ponds and lakes in cold areas of the world acts as an insulating barrier that protects the aquatic life below. If ice were denser than liquid water, ice forming on a pond would sink, thereby exposing more water to the cold temperature. Thus, the pond would eventually freeze throughout, killing all the life-forms present.[34]

The wonders of God's creation has me baffled and at the same time in awe. The suspension of the planets, the moon, the sun, and stars are amazingly phenomenal. The multitude of species of orchids and their resemblance to animal life is stunning. Just knowing how big and heavy an eagle and an airplane can be, yet the bald eagle smoothly soars high and beautifully, while a plane can lift off into the

---

[34] https://www.britannica.com/science/water

sky with so much weight and yet travel above the clouds. The foresight of God when He created water, an entity we need to survive. Truly, there is a God.

 CHAPTER

6

How to Live Freely

In Galatians 5:1, we are called to be free, stand firm, and not waiver. The goal is to be free from the bondage of sin, which can only come by accepting Jesus Christ as our Savior and Lord. It is a gift given to us by the grace of God to everyone who puts their faith in Him. Once we accept that Jesus Christ paid the price for our sin and submit to His will, sinful habits will begin to diminish. Our actions and thoughts to obey God and walking in a personal relationship with God and Jesus Christ will enable us to strive to live in righteousness and thus be free from sin. This is not to say that we will never stumble and fall again, but instead, we will get up and repent to move forward and to live freely in peace with God.

> *It is for freedom that Christ has set us free. Stand firm, then, and do not let yourselves be burdened again by a yoke of slavery.*
> *Galatians 5:1*
> *New International Version (NIV)*

In the Book of Galatians 1:6-9, Paul was warning the Galatian Christians not to return to the practices of the Law and the dependency on Judaism for salvation. Basically, he was telling them not to go back to old religious traditions. False preaching was being spread, raising disputes, controversies, and it was confusing the Galatian Christians. The false preaching was trying to pervert the Gospel of Christ by mixing in need of works for salvation. Also, in the book of Philippians 3:2-3, we are warned of evil workers, legalistic Jews who were preaching that along with the need to believe and accept Jesus, they were including the old traditions of circumcision of the flesh and works as a need for salvation. This is why Paul was defending the Gospel of Jesus Christ when he said:

> *I am astonished that you are so quickly deserting the one who called you to live in the grace of Christ and are turning to a different gospel — which is really no gospel at all. Evidently some people are throwing you into confusion and are trying to pervert the gospel of Christ. But even if we or an angel from heaven should preach a gospel other than the one we preached to you, let them be under God's curse! As we have already said, so now I say again: If anybody is preaching to you a gospel other than what you accepted, let them be under God's curse!*
>
> *Galatians 1:6-9*
> *New International Version (NIV)*

> *Watch out for those dogs, those evildoers, those mutilators of the flesh. "For it is we who are the circumcision, we who serve God by his Spirit, who boast in Christ Jesus, and who put no confidence in the flesh"*
>
> *Philippians 3:2-3*
> *New International Version (NIV)*

This freedom is not to be used to indulge in earthly pleasures but in humbly serving, loving God, and fellow brothers and sisters; see Galatians 5:13.

> *You, my brothers and sisters, were called to be free. But do not use your freedom to indulge the flesh; rather, serve one another humbly in love.*
>
> *Galatians 5:13*
> *New International Version (NIV).*

God gave man the desire to seek Him and the instructions for living a righteous, prosperous, and fulfilled life found throughout the scriptures. With everything handed to Adam and Eve, they were not content, and when offered more, the devil easily trapped them by misleading them regarding the truths God had given them. The devil will manipulate the word of God to trap and deceive people to live an ungodly life by making earthly ways seem attractive. Even Jesus was tempted by the serpent by misusing the word of God. We are not to use or manipulate the word for our gain but to seek the truth. Unlike Adam and Eve, we have many opportunities to learn and understand what it is like to live a free life. To learn and understand the will of God, one can solicit the guidance and counseling from a Pastor, Christian friend, or Christian family member, by reading the Bible, and by being attentive when God speaks to us through circumstances and our thoughts. Proverbs is filled with instructions for numerous life situations, such as the pattern for working rather than being lazy, as seen in Proverbs 6:6-11, and with wise sayings and teachings for living with wisdom under the authority of God, see Proverbs 2:1-6.

> *Go to the ant, you sluggard; consider its ways and be wise! It has no commander, no overseer or ruler, yet it stores its provisions in summer and gathers its food at harvest. How long will you lie there, you sluggard?*
>
> *When will you get up from your sleep? A little sleep, a little slumber, a little folding of the hands to rest — and poverty will come on you like a thief and scarcity like an armed man.*
>
> *Proverbs 6:6-11*
New International Version (NIV)

> *My son, if you receive my words and treasure up my commandments with you, making your ear attentive to wisdom and inclining your heart to understanding; yes, if you call out for insight and raise your voice for understanding, if you seek it like silver and search for it as for hidden treasures, then you will understand the fear of the Lord and find*

> *the knowledge of God. For the Lord gives wisdom; from his mouth come knowledge and understanding.*
>
> *Proverbs 2:1-6*
> *English Standard Version (ESV)*

The word "fear" found in the Bible has many meanings from having reverence and respect towards God to fearing in terror of judgment, hell, wrath, and destruction. When we fear the Lord, we will hate evil, as seen in Proverbs 8:13. In Proverbs 1:2-7, fear means reverence for and obedience to God, and it is the beginning of knowledge. It is an attitude of respect, wanting to please and love God. It is a holy, humble submission to the Word of God and fear of God with devotion by obeying His teachings.

> *To fear the Lord is to hate evil; I hate pride and arrogance, evil behavior and perverse speech.*
>
> *Proverbs 8:13*
> *New International Version (NIV)*

> *To know wisdom and instruction, to understand words of insight, to receive instruction in wise dealing, in righteousness, justice, and equity; to give prudence to the simple, knowledge and discretion to the youth—Let the wise hear and increase in learning, and the one who understands obtain guidance, to understand a proverb and a saying, the words of the wise and their*

> *riddles. The fear of the Lord is the beginning of knowledge.*
>
> *Proverbs 1:2-7*
> *English Standard Version (ESV)*

Colossians 3:12-17 teaches us the principals for a righteous life such as setting our heart and mind on things that are above and thus putting to death the old self, earthly nature:

> *Therefore, as God's chosen people, holy and dearly loved, clothe yourselves with compassion, kindness, humility, gentleness and patience. Bear with each other and forgive one another if any of you has a grievance against someone. Forgive as the Lord forgave you. And over all these virtues put on love, which binds them all together in perfect unity. Let the peace of Christ rule in your hearts, since as members of one body you were called to peace. And be thankful. Let the message of Christ dwell among you richly as you teach and admonish one another with all wisdom through psalms, hymns, and songs from the Spirit, singing to God with gratitude in your hearts. And whatever you do, whether in word or deed, do it all in the name of the Lord Jesus, giving thanks to God the Father through him.*
>
> *Colossians 3:12-17*
> *New International Version (NIV)*

The law of the spirit of life, which is the gospel or good news of Jesus Christ, is the only way to eternal salvation. According to Romans 8:1-4, the law of the spirit has set you free, and there is no condemnation for those in Christ Jesus. The law of the spirit refers to the guidance of the Holy Spirit, who empowers us to live in righteousness with wisdom to overcome worldly desires.

> *There is therefore now no condemnation for those who are in Christ Jesus. For the law of the Spirit of life has set you free in Christ Jesus from the law of sin and death. For God has done what the law, weakened by the flesh, could not do. By sending his own Son in the likeness of sinful flesh and for sin, he condemned sin in the flesh, in order that the righteous requirement of the law might be fulfilled in us, who walk not according to the flesh but according to the Spirit.*
>
> *Romans 8:1-4*
> *English Standard Version (ESV)*

Christ crucifixion was in lieu of us being crucified so that we could live in Christ as He was the only one who could pay the price once and for all. Galatians 2:20 and Romans 6:5-16 records that we have been crucified with Christ. To say one is crucified with Christ means that our old self, worldly living, and sinful ways have died, but instead, we live in the ways instructed in the scriptures, that is a righteous living; thus, we are dead to sin and alive to God:

I have been crucified with Christ. It is no longer I who live, but Christ who lives in me. And the life I now live in the flesh I live by faith in the Son of God, who loved me and gave himself for me.

Galatians 2:20
English Standard Version (ESV)

For if we have been united with him in a death like his, we shall certainly be united with him in a resurrection like his. We know that our old self was crucified with him in order that the body of sin might be brought to nothing, so that we would no longer be enslaved to sin. For one who has died has been set free from sin. Now if we have died with Christ, we believe that we will also live with him. We know that Christ, being raised from the dead, will never die again; death no longer has dominion over him. For the death he died he died to sin, once for all, but the life he lives he lives to God. So you also must consider yourselves dead to sin and alive to God in Christ Jesus. Let not sin therefore reign in your mortal body, to make you obey its passions. Do not present your members to sin as instruments for unrighteousness, but present yourselves to God as those who have been brought from death to life, and your members to God as instruments for righteousness. For sin will have no dominion over you, since you are not under law but under grace.

Slaves to Righteousness What then? Are we to sin because we are not under law but under grace? By no means! Do you not know that if you present yourselves to anyone as obedient slaves, you are slaves of the one whom you obey, either of sin, which leads to death, or of obedience, which leads to righteousness?
Romans 6:5-16
English Standard Version (ESV)

CHAPTER

7

Living a Christian Life

Living a Christian life means being born again as salvation is the first step for living a Christian Life, and the best example is to follow the teaching Jesus commanded and demonstrated.

- Being Born Again

Born again is a spiritual rebirth, which means we have faith in Jesus Christ and will daily walk personally with God. We mentally and wholeheartedly choose to give ourselves by being obedient to God. In John 3:3 and John 14:6, Jesus tells us of the need to be born again, that is, to be born again into a living hope to be saved and have eternal life in Jesus Christ. In 1Peter 1:3, we see God's mercy for our assurance of eternal life through the death and resurrection of Jesus Christ. In 2Corinthians 5:17 and Ephesians 4:17-25, Jesus was not only telling the people but was insisting that they were not to live unrighteously because they are new creatures and no longer living in the flesh but living in righteousness.

Jesus replied, "Very truly I tell you, no one can see the kingdom of God unless they are born again."

John 3:3
New International Version (NIV)

Jesus answered, "I am the way and the truth and the life. No one comes to the Father except through me.

John 14:6
New International Version (NIV)

Blessed be the God and Father of our Lord Jesus Christ! According to his great mercy, he has caused us to be born again to a living hope through the resurrection of Jesus Christ from the dead.

1 Peter 1:3
English Standard Version (ESV)

Therefore, if anyone is in Christ, he is a new creation. The old has passed away; behold, the new has come.

2 Corinthians 5:17
English Standard Version (ESV)

So I tell you this, and insist on it in the Lord, that you must no longer live as the Gentiles do, in the futility of their thinking. They are darkened in their understanding and separated from the life of God because of the

> *ignorance that is in them due to the hardening of their hearts. Having lost all sensitivity, they have given themselves over to sensuality so as to indulge in every kind of impurity, and they are full of greed. That, however, is not the way of life you learned when you heard about Christ and were taught in him in accordance with the truth that is in Jesus. You were taught, with regard to your former way of life, to put off your old self, which is being corrupted by its deceitful desires; to be made new in the attitude of your minds; and to put on the new self, created to be like God in true righteousness and holiness. Therefore, each of you must put off falsehood and speak truthfully to your neighbor, for we are all members of one body.*
>
> *Ephesians 4:17-25*
> *New International Version (NIV)*

- Access to God

When Jesus was crucified, He loudly spoke His last words, and when He took His last breath, the inner veil that concealed the Ark of the Covenant, which was made of blue and purple and scarlet yarns and fine twined linen, was split in half from top to bottom. This gave access to God through Jesus before the veil splitting in half; only the High Priest could enter the Holy of Holies and only once a year. See Matthew 27:50-51 and Exodus 26:31-33.

> *And when Jesus had cried out again in a loud voice, he gave up his spirit. At that moment the curtain of the temple was torn in two from top to bottom.*
>
> *Matthew 27:50-51*
> *New International Version (NIV)*

> *Make a curtain of blue, purple and scarlet yarn and finely twisted linen, with cherubim woven into it by a skilled worker. Hang it with gold hooks on four posts of acacia wood overlaid with gold and standing on four silver bases. Hang the curtain from the clasps and place the ark of the covenant law behind the curtain. The curtain will separate the Holy Place from the Most Holy Place.*
>
> *Exodus 26:31-33*
> *New International Version (NIV)*

Once saved by accepting Jesus, our journey in living a Christian life begins, and we have access to God through faith in Jesus. Romans 5:2, Hebrews 10:19-22, Ephesians 2:18, and Ephesians 3:11-12 remind us that we have obtained access to God since we have been washed with the blood of Jesus; and now have the freedom and confidence to approach God.

Everywhere, people are using cell phones to keep in contact with their business associates, friends, or family. Unlike a cell phone in which the battery can die, or we step out of a cell towers radio signal, which can break our communication,

communication with God is never broken unless we are the one to step away. We have the freedom to communicate with God as He is always available, and He is interested in every detail of your life.

> *Through him we have also obtained access by faith into this grace in which we stand, and we rejoice in hope of the glory of God.*
> *Romans 5:2*
> *English Standard Version (ESV)*

> *Therefore, brothers and sisters, since we have confidence to enter the Most Holy Place by the blood of Jesus, by a new and living way opened for us through the curtain, that is, his body, and since we have a great priest over the house of God, let us draw near to God with a sincere heart and with the full assurance that faith brings, having our hearts sprinkled to cleanse us from a guilty conscience and having our bodies washed with pure water.*
> *Hebrews 10:19-22*
> *New International Version (NIV)*

> *For through him we both have access to the Father by one Spirit.*
> *Ephesians 2:18*
> *New International Version (NIV)*

> *According to his eternal purpose that he accomplished in Christ Jesus our Lord.*

> *In him and through faith in him we may approach God with freedom and confidence.*
> *Ephesians 3:11-12*
> *New International Version (NIV)*

- Heart and Mind of Christ

Principles for living in righteousness begins with our thoughts and heart as we move away from bad influences and worldly habits, see Romans 12:2. We need to change our way of thinking, which will enable us to decipher the difference between worldly thinking and righteousness. While the world says it is okay to falsely slander someone's character, the Bible instructs us in James 4:11-12 not to slander a brother or sister; instead, we are to uplift and encourage one another. Too often, people curse out of habit as this becomes acceptable in our society, but in Ephesians 4:29, we are not to use unwholesome words but only what benefits the listener. Mark 7:20-23 reminds us that out of the heart comes evil thoughts. In Isaiah 55:7, we are to forsake the way of an evil life as God will forgive our sins when we call on Him, and in Ephesians 4:23, we are made new and need to change the attitude of our mind.

> *Do not conform to the pattern of this world, but be transformed by the renewing of your mind. Then you will be able to test and approve what God's will is —his good, pleasing and perfect will.*
> *Romans 12:2*
> *New International Version (NIV)*

Brothers and sisters, do not slander one another. Anyone who speaks against a brother or sister or judges them speaks against the law and judges it. When you judge the law, you are not keeping it, but sitting in judgment on it. There is only one Lawgiver and Judge, the one who is able to save and destroy. But you—who are you to judge your neighbor?
James 4:11-12
New International Version (NIV)

Do not let any unwholesome talk come out of your mouths, but only what is helpful for building others up according to their needs, that it may benefit those who listen.
Ephesians 4:29
New International Version (NIV)

And he said, "What comes out of a person is what defiles him. For from within, out of the heart of man, come evil thoughts, sexual immorality, theft, murder, adultery, coveting, wickedness, deceit, sensuality, envy, slander, pride, foolishness. All these evil things come from within, and they defile a person."
Mark 7:20-23
English Standard Version (ESV)

Let the wicked forsake his way, and the unrighteous man his thoughts; let him return to the Lord, that he may have compassion on him, and to our God, for he will abundantly pardon.

Isaiah 55:7
English Standard Version (ESV)

To be made new in the attitude of your minds; and to put on the new self, created to be like God in true righteousness and holiness.

Ephesians 4:23
New International Version (NIV)

- Love through Action

Practice love through action, sincerely, and with a joyful heart. We are called to reconcile with one another by praying for even our enemy, work together, and help our brothers and sisters in need when the opportunity arises. It is not necessary to wait to help someone when the need is big but daily exercise to help someone with the small things in life. Encouragement and showing love can be as simple as paying for someone's morning beverage or helping someone struggling to get into a car due to physical limitations. The little things in life can often start a person's day in the right direction to be happier and with a positive attitude. When able, assist in encouraging others with the bigger issues of life. As Jesus laid down his life for us, we are to be willing to lay down our life for a friend. Our military and first responders are good examples of people willing to lay down their life for another. Love in actions with a sincere attitude is evident when one is devoted to others in love;

this is stated in the following verses, Romans 12:9-13, John 15:12-14, Matthew 5:44-45, and John 13:1.

> *Love must be sincere. Hate what is evil; cling to what is good. Be devoted to one another in love. Honor one another above yourselves. Never be lacking in zeal, but keep your spiritual fervor, serving the Lord. Be joyful in hope, patient in affliction, faithful in prayer. Share with the Lord's people who are in need. Practice hospitality.*
>
> *Romans 12:9-13*
> *New International Version (NIV)*

> *My command is this: Love each other as I have loved you. Greater love has no one than this: to lay down one's life for one's friends. You are my friends if you do what I command.*
>
> *John 15:12-14*
> *New International Version (NIV)*

> *But I tell you, love your enemies and pray for those who persecute you, that you may be children of your Father in heaven. He causes his sun to rise on the evil and the good, and sends rain on the righteous and the unrighteous.*
>
> *Matthew 5:44-45*
> *New International Version (NIV)*

> *It was just before the Passover Festival. Jesus knew that the hour had come for him to leave this world and go to the Father. Having loved his own who were in the world, he loved them to the end.*
>
> *John 13:1*
> *New International Version (NIV)*

- Seek the Good in Others

As Christian, we are to seek the good of others, putting others above ourselves and to do this with humility so they may be saved, see 1Corinthians 10:23-24, Philippians 2:21, Romans 12:10, and Philippians 2:3-4. Seeking the good in others can be a powerful tool not only for the other person's life but within our own life, as this builds confidence, love, and encouragement. When building up others, their self-esteem, and how they value themselves dramatically increase. Thus, they become more productive and happier. See 1 Thessalonians 5:1. In a world where we find ourselves rushing in every direction, it is sometimes hard to slow down and get acquainted with others beyond the "Hi and How are you" stage. Seek the good in others to complement the positives by being aware of their strengths; for example, they may be talented, wise, generous, show kindness and patience, or they may be honest people.

> *"I have the right to do anything," you say— but not everything is beneficial. "I have the right to do anything"—but not everything is*

constructive. No one should seek their own good, but the good of others.
1 Corinthians 10:23-24
New International Version (NIV)

Even as I try to please everyone in every way. For I am not seeking my own good but the good of many, so that they may be saved.
1 Corinthians 10:33
New International Version (NIV)

For everyone looks out for their own interests, not those of Jesus Christ.
Philippians 2:21
New International Version (NIV)

Be devoted to one another in love. Honor one another above yourselves.
Romans 12:10
New International Version (NIV)

Do nothing out of selfish ambition or vain conceit. Rather, in humility value others above yourselves, not looking to your own interests but each of you to the interests of the others.
Philippians 2:3-4
New International Version (NIV)

Therefore encourage one another and build each other up, just as in fact you are doing.
1 Thessalonians 5:11
New International Version (NIV)

Make every effort to live in peace with everyone.

Hebrews 12:14
New International Version (NIV)

- Supplication

Supplication, also referred to as petitioning, is humbly praying for one's needs or on behalf of another.

The definition of Supplication, according to Dictionary Definition - Supplication vocabulary.com is:

> *Although it is a noun, supplication comes from the Latin verb supplicare, which means "to plead humbly." While a supplication is often thought of as a religious prayer (it is used 60 times in the Bible), it can logically be applied to any situation in which you must entreat someone in power for help or a favor.[35]*

While making our request known to God with a humble spirit, we need to yield to God, allowing Him to change our way of thinking to lineup with His will.

> Like in the song, *The Potters Hand,* we should be asking God to, "Take me, Mold me, Use me, Fill me I give my life to the Potter's hands."

---

[35] https://www.vocabulary.com/dictionary/supplication

Let God shape you into who He wants you to be; see Jeremiah 18:3-4. In Isaiah 64:8, we are compared to clay in the potter's hand, the work of His hands. An open mind to the call of God will help us walk closer to Him and be willing to follow Jesus's examples for the way we should live. In 1Thessalonians 5:16, we are reminded to continually pray and give thanks as this is the will of God. God invites us to ask for help and advice for ourselves and for others in need; this is found in Matthew 7:7-8. In James 4:2-3, we are reminded that we do not have because we do not ask. God's doors are open, and He is waiting for His children to come to Him for help. Pray for the world (peace, hunger, and salvation for the lost), family, and friends see Ephesians 6:18. God already knows the needs of His children, but we are to pray, and by praying, we are inviting God into our lives, and at the same time, this keeps us in fellowship with Him. Philippians 4:6 reminds us to pray and not be anxious about anything because God wants to answer our supplication, our cries for help.

> *Go down to the potter's house, and there I will give you my message." So I went down to the potter's house, and I saw him working at the wheel. But the pot he was shaping from the clay was marred in his hands; so the potter formed it into another pot, shaping it as seemed best to him.*
>
> *Jeremiah 18:3-4*
> *New International Version (NIV)*

Yet you, Lord, are our Father. We are the clay, you are the potter; we are all the work of your hand.

Isaiah 64:8
New International Version (NIV)

Rejoice always, pray continually, give thanks in all circumstances; for this is God's will for you in Christ Jesus.

1 Thessalonians 5:16-18
New International Version (NIV)

Ask and it will be given to you; seek and you will find; knock and the door will be opened to you. For everyone who asks receives; the one who seeks finds; and to the one who knocks, the door will be opened.

Matthew 7:7-8
New International Version (NIV)

You do not have because you do not ask God.
James 4:2-3
New International Version (NIV)

And pray in the Spirit on all occasions with all kinds of prayers and requests. With this in mind, be alert and always keep on praying for all the Lord's people.

Ephesians 6:18
New International Version (NIV)

> *Do not be anxious about anything, but in every situation, by prayer and petition, with thanksgiving, present your requests to God.*
> *Philippians 4:6*
> *New International Version (NIV)*

- Show Humility

Humble yourself as you seek the Lord's will and be willing to put others first. Ephesians 4:2 and James 4:13 remind us to be humble and gentle before the Lord. Jesus showed humility when He surrendered His will to be obedient and faithful to the Father's will. He came in human form, He was a servant versus coming to be served, and He humbled Himself to the extent of dying a crucial death on the cross. See Philippians 2:5-8 and Matthew 26:39. Likewise, we are to show humility towards others, as this creates unity. Our attitude should be to respect others above ourselves.

I had opportunities to train new and young employees with Master's degrees seeking upper management positions. Training these young adults showed humility as they were willing to listen to a less educated person and not think of themselves as better. Often, I would tell them that in this field of work, there was more than one way to get the same results (especially when using the computer); therefore, they were to listen and observe other opinions to make a wise choice. In the same way, we must not think that our opinion is the only and right way. 1 Peter 5:5-7 instructs the younger generation to respect and humble themselves before elders, and we are all to be humble towards others.

Be completely humble and gentle; be patient, bearing with one another in love.

Ephesians 4:2
New International Version (NIV)

Humble yourselves before the Lord, and he will lift you up.

James 4:13
New International Version (NIV)

Rather, he made himself nothing by taking the very nature of a servant, being made in human likeness. And being found in appearance as a man, he humbled himself by becoming obedient to death — even death on a cross!

Philippians 2:5-8
New International Version (NIV)

Going a little farther, he fell with his face to the ground and prayed, "My Father, if it is possible, may this cup be taken from me. Yet not as I will, but as you will."

Matthew 26:39
New International Version (NIV)

In the same way, you who are younger, submit yourselves to your elders. All of you, clothe yourselves with humility toward one another, because, "God opposes the proud but shows favor to the humble." Humble yourselves,

> *therefore, under God's mighty hand, that he may lift you up in due time. Cast all your anxiety on him because he cares for you.*
>
> *1 Peter 5:5-7*
> *New International Version (NIV)*

- Have a Servant's Attitude

Jesus became a servant because of His love and wanting to be obedient to His father; the motivation was rooted in unselfish and heartfelt affection. Everyone is of great value to Him, and He reached out to those that people looked upon as untouchable or unclean, like those with leprosy. Many verses in the Bible reports Jesus as a servant, such as in Matthew 20:28, Mark 10:45, Luke 22:27, and Ephesians 2:10.

> *Just as the Son of Man did not come to be served, but to serve, and to give his life as a ransom for many."*
>
> *Matthew 20:28*
> *New International Version (NIV)*
>
> *For even the Son of Man did not come to be served, but to serve, and to give his life as a ransom for many.*
>
> *Mark 10:45*
> *New International Version (NIV)*
>
> *For who is greater, the one who is at the table or the one who serves? Is it not the one who*

is at the table? But I am among you as one who serves.

Luke 22:27
New International Version (NIV)

For we are God's handiwork, created in Christ Jesus to do good works, which God prepared in advance for us to do.

Ephesians 2:10
New International Version (NIV)

Jesus not only told his disciples that they needed to be a servant, but He showed them through His actions. In the book of John 13:1-17, Jesus washed his disciples' feet and dried them with the towel that was wrapped around His waist. Jesus washing the disciples' feet is an example of servanthood and humility. When humbled, one seeks God's approval rather than man's approval; thus, serving comes from humility and not out of a selfish attitude. Jesus said to the disciple that they would be blessed if they followed His examples by humbling themselves and servicing one another.

> *It was just before the Passover Festival. Jesus knew that the hour had come for him to leave this world and go to the Father. Having loved his own who were in the world, he loved them to the end. The evening meal was in progress, and the devil had already prompted Judas, the son of Simon Iscariot, to betray Jesus. Jesus knew that the Father had put all things under his power, and that he had come from*

God and was returning to God; so he got up from the meal, took off his outer clothing, and wrapped a towel around his waist. After that, he poured water into a basin and began to wash his disciples' feet, drying them with the towel that was wrapped around him. He came to Simon Peter, who said to him, "Lord, are you going to wash my feet?" Jesus replied, "You do not realize now what I am doing, but later you will understand." "No," said Peter, "you shall never wash my feet." Jesus answered, "Unless I wash you, you have no part with me." "Then, Lord," Simon Peter replied, "not just my feet but my hands and my head as well!" Jesus answered, "Those who have had a bath need only to wash their feet; their whole body is clean. And you are clean, though not every one of you." For he knew who was going to betray him, and that was why he said not every one was clean. When he had finished washing their feet, he put on his clothes and returned to his place. "Do you understand what I have done for you?" he asked them. "You call me 'Teacher' and 'Lord,' and rightly so, for that is what I am. Now that I, your Lord and Teacher, have washed your feet, you also should wash one another's feet. I have set you an example that you should do as I have done for you. Very truly I tell you, no servant is greater than his master, nor is a messenger greater than the

> *one who sent him. Now that you know these things, you will be blessed if you do them.*
>
> *John 13:1-17*
> *New International Version (NIV)*

Servanthood should come from genuinely caring for others by seeking opportunities or when prompted by the Holy Spirit to express love through action. As stated before, small acts of kindness go a long way in creating peace and encouraging others.

- Confess Sins

Confess all your sins, known and unknown, seeking forgiveness to clean the slate as God has promised to forgive and forget, see Isaiah 43:25, Acts 3:19, and 1 John 1:9. Confess with the intention of not being a repeat offender. Since Jesus is the only one that is sinless, and we are prone to sin because we are born with a sinful nature, it is important to confess our sin every time we sin. God will wash away our offenses and forgive us. When we sin, our fellowship with God is separated, see Isaiah 59:2, as He does not tolerate sin, but by confessing our sins, our fellowship is restored because of the blood of Jesus Christ.

> *I, even I, am he who blots out your transgressions, for my own sake, and remembers your sins no more.*
>
> *Isaiah 43:25*
> *New International Version (NIV)*

Repent, then, and turn to God, so that your sins may be wiped out, that times of refreshing may come from the Lord.
Acts 3:19
New International Version (NIV)

If we confess our sins, he is faithful and just and will forgive us our sins and purify us from all unrighteousness.
1 John 1:9
New International Version (NIV)

But your iniquities have separated you from your God; your sins have hidden his face from you, so that he will not hear.
Isaiah 59:2
New International Version (NIV)

CHAPTER

8

Follow Jesus' Example

- Pray Without Ceasing

Rejoice always and continually find the time to pray with adoration and gratitude, as prayer is a privilege. As Christians, we have a God that is always ready to hear and communicate with us. In Mark 1:35, Jesus began His day praying in a solitary place, and He was up while it was dark. In 1Thessalonians 5:16-18, we are to pray without ceasing, which means to consciously be aware that God is with us all the time. Pray throughout the day while working, thanking God for the opportunity to work and earn a living rather than the alternative of being unemployed and destitute. While performing chores, pray for others' needs about illness, finances, relationships, or whatever the Lord brings to your mind. Performing chores around the house means you have been blessed with shelter and protection from the outside elements. Quite often, we find ourselves waiting; this is a good time to pray and listen in the quietness of God's presence. Jesus took the time away from the crowds to pray to His Father, see Matthew 26:36 and Luke 5:16. While in basic military training, my son said, "We are rushed just to wait", this would be a great time to pray. We are to pray by praising God, worshiping and honoring God as our Lord of lords, King of kings, Almighty God, and Lord over all, see Psalm 136:2-3.

> *Very early in the morning, while it was still dark, Jesus got up, left the house and went off to a solitary place, where he prayed.*
> *Mark 1:35*
> *New International Version (NIV)*

> *Rejoice always, pray continually, give thanks in all circumstances; for this is God's will for you in Christ Jesus.*
> *1 Thessalonians 5:16-18*
> *New International Version (NIV)*

> *Then Jesus went with his disciples to a place called Gethsemane, and he said to them, "Sit here while I go over there and pray."*
> *Matthew 26:36*
> *New International Version (NIV)*

> *But Jesus often withdrew to lonely places and prayed.*
> *Luke 5:16*
> *New International Version (NIV)*

> *Give thanks to the God of gods. His love endures forever. Give thanks to the Lord of lords: His love endures forever.*
>
> *Psalm 136:2-3*
> *New International Version (NIV)*

- Thank God

Verbally give thanks for everything God has provided for you and others. God graciously gives, so we should always be grateful. There were several occasions recorded in the Bible in which Jesus thankfully prayed to God the Father. Below is an example of Jesus praying to His Father in Matthew 11:25. Jesus prayed to the Father when God revealed the doctrine of the gospel to only a few people. The doctrine was hidden from those that considered themselves to be wise and prudent in their own conceit as they were wise in worldly matters. The little children refer to babe-like men, the meek and helpless, those seeking the truths in Godly matters.

> *The Father Revealed in the Son: At that time Jesus said, "I praise you, Father, Lord of heaven and earth, because you have hidden these things from the wise and learned, and revealed them to little children.*
>
> *Matthew 11:25*
> *New International Version (NIV)*

John Gill's Bible Study Tools explains what Jesus meant when he prayed, "Because thou hast hid these things from the wise and prudent."

Because thou hast hid these things from the wise and prudent.

> *The "things" he means are the doctrines of the Gospel; such as respect himself, his person, as God, and the Son of God; his office, as Messiah, Redeemer, and Saviour; and the blessings of grace, righteousness, and salvation by him. The persons from whom these things were hid, are "the wise and prudent"; in things worldly, natural, and civil; men of great parts and learning, of a large compass of knowledge, having a considerable share of sagacity, penetration, and wisdom; or, at least, who were wise and prudent in their own conceits, as were the Scribes and Pharisees, and the schools of Hillell and Shammai, the two famous doctors of that day: and indeed the people of the Jews in common were so; who thus applaud themselves at the eating of the passover every year, and say, "we are all wise, we are all prudent, we all understand the law"; the same is elsewhere said of all Israel; in their opinion they were so, yet the things of the Gospel are hidden from them.[36]*

In John 6:10-13 and Mark 6:37-44, Jesus fed five thousand people that were seated while at the Sea of Galilee with just five barley loaves and two fish. Before they ate, Jesus took

---

[36] https://www.biblestudytools.com/commentaries/gills-exposition-of-the-bible/matthew-11-25.html

the loaves and fish and thanked God. When everyone was satisfied, there were twelve baskets full of leftover pieces of bread and fish. Likewise, on another occasion, Jesus fed another crowd which is recorded in Mark 8:1-2. Jesus gave thanks to God before they ate. There were four thousand people and seven loaves and a few small fish; when everyone had plenty to eat, the disciples collected seven baskets full of broken bread and fish.

> *Jesus said, "Have the people sit down." There was plenty of grass in that place, and they sat down (about five thousand men were there). Jesus then took the loaves, gave thanks, and distributed to those who were seated as much as they wanted. He did the same with the fish. When they had all had enough to eat, he said to his disciples, "Gather the pieces that are left over. Let nothing be wasted." So they gathered them and filled twelve baskets with the pieces of the five barley loaves left over by those who had eaten.*
>
> *John 6:10-13*
> *New International Version (NIV)*

> *But he answered, "You give them something to eat." They said to him, "That would take more than half a year's wages! Are we to go and spend that much on bread and give it to them to eat?" "How many loaves do you have?" he asked. "Go and see." When they found out, they said, "Five—and two fish."*

Then Jesus directed them to have all the people sit down in groups on the green grass. So they sat down in groups of hundreds and fifties. Taking the five loaves and the two fish and looking up to heaven, he gave thanks and broke the loaves. Then he gave them to his disciples to distribute to the people. He also divided the two fish among them all. They all ate and were satisfied, and the disciples picked up twelve basketfuls of broken pieces of bread and fish. The number of the men who had eaten was five thousand.

Mark 6:37-44
New International Version (NIV)

During those days another large crowd gathered. Since they had nothing to eat, Jesus called his disciples to him and said, "I have compassion for these people; they have already been with me three days and have nothing to eat. If I send them home hungry, they will collapse on the way, because some of them have come a long distance." His disciples answered, "But where in this remote place can anyone get enough bread to feed them?" "How many loaves do you have?" Jesus asked. "Seven," they replied. He told the crowd to sit down on the ground. When he had taken the seven loaves and given thanks, he broke them and gave them to his disciples to distribute to the people, and they did so. They had a few small fish as well; he gave thanks for them also and told the disciples to distribute them. The people ate and were satisfied. Afterward the disciples picked up seven basketfuls of broken pieces that were left over. About four thousand were present.

Mark 8:1-9
New International Version (NIV)

The books of Matthew, Mark, and Luke record the events of the Last Supper, the last meal Jesus had with his disciples before the crucifixion. On the first day of the Festival of Unleavened Bread, at the Passover, it was customary to sacrifice the Passover lamb. While Jesus and the disciples were eating, Jesus began to pray, giving thanks instructing the disciples to eat of the bread and drink of the wine as a reminder of Jesus' body and blood offered up for them. These instructions were not only for the disciples but for all times. The account of the Last Supper as recorded in Luke 22:7-20 is a follow:

Then came the day of Unleavened Bread on which the Passover lamb had to be sacrificed. Jesus sent Peter and John, saying, "Go and make preparations for us to eat the Passover." "Where do you want us to prepare for it?" they asked.

He replied, "As you enter the city, a man carrying a jar of water will meet you. Follow him to the house that he enters, and say to the owner of the house, 'The Teacher asks:

Where is the guest room, where I may eat the Passover with my disciples?' He will show you a large room upstairs, all furnished. Make preparations there." They left and found things just as Jesus had told them. So they prepared the Passover. When the hour came, Jesus and his apostles reclined at the table. And he said to them, "I have eagerly desired to eat this Passover with you before I suffer. For I tell you, I will not eat it again until it finds fulfillment in the kingdom of God." After taking the cup, he gave thanks and said, "Take this and divide it among you. For I tell you I will not drink again from the fruit of the vine until the kingdom of God comes." And he took bread, gave thanks and broke it, and gave it to them, saying, "This is my body given for you; do this in remembrance of me." In the same way, after the supper he took the cup, saying, "This cup is the new covenant in my blood, which is poured out for you.

Luke 22:17-20
New International Version (NIV)

- Forgive

Be forgiving, kind, tenderhearted, and compassionate to everyone as they may be in the middle of enduring trials that we may not be aware of; therefore, treat others as you would like to be treated, see Ephesians 4:32. It is important to forgive others as we are fully forgiven of our sins when we repent. As stated in Matthew 6:14-15 and Mark 11:25, if we want to be forgiven by our heavenly Father, we must forgive others. When we forgive someone, we are to rid ourselves from bitterness and every form of malice, not holding anything against them; see Ephesians 4:31.

> *Be kind and compassionate to one another, forgiving each other, just as in Christ God forgave you.*
>
> *Ephesians 4:32*
> *New International Version (NIV)*

> *For if you forgive other people when they sin against you, your heavenly Father will also forgive you. But if you do not forgive others their sins, your Father will not forgive your sins.*
>
> *Matthew 6:14-15*
> *New International Version (NIV)*

> *if you hold anything against anyone, forgive them, so that your Father in heaven may forgive you your sins."*
>
> *Mark 11:25*
> *New International Version (NIV)*

> *Get rid of all bitterness, rage and anger, brawling and slander, along with every form of malice.*
>
> *Ephesians 4:31*
> *New International Version (NIV)*

When unjustly hurt by others, give this burden to God by forgiving the offender as this releases the strain of carrying bitterness and anger. Allowing bitterness to stir up within us only exposes us to problems that can hurt us physically and mentally. In following Jesus' example, we need to extend to others grace, free and undeserved help, love, and mercy. When we forgive, we are not saying that what they did was okay, and we are not condoning or excusing what the other person may have done; instead, we are choosing to release resentment.

According to crosswalk.com, in the article: What Does the Bible Say About Forgiveness? There are healthy benefits:

> Studies have found that the act of forgiveness can reap huge rewards for your health, lowering the risk of heart attack; improving cholesterol levels and sleep; and reducing pain, blood pressure, and levels of anxiety, depression and stress. And research points to an increase in the forgiveness-health connection as you age."[37]

Forgiving those that hurt us means we are to make sure we set boundaries by holding others accountable for their actions, and thus not allowing them to continue hurting us. There are times when it may be necessary to sever our ties with them. The main point is to forgive as God in Christ

---

[37] https://www.crosswalk.com/faith/bible-study/what-does-the-bible-say-about-forgiveness.html

forgives us. Several verses regarding forgiveness are found in Colossians 3:13, Matthew 7:12, and Luke 6:31:

> *Bear with each other and forgive one another if any of you has a grievance against someone. Forgive as the Lord forgave you.*
>
> *Colossians 3:13*
> *New International Version (NIV)*

> *So in everything, do to others what you would have them do to you, for this sums up the Law and the Prophets.*
>
> *Matthew 7:12*
> *New International Version (NIV)*

> *Do to others as you would have them do to you.*
>
> *Luke 6:31*
> *New International Version (NIV)*

- Share the Gospel to Everyone

Christians are commissioned to share and proclaim the teachings of Jesus Christ to a lost world, just as Jesus ministered to everyone throughout His journey. In the following scriptures, we are commanded to go into the world and make disciples in every nation, baptizing in the name of the Father, the Son, and the Holy Spirit. This is found in Mark 16:15, Matthew 28:19-20, and Psalm 96:3. God uses everyone willing to accept His call, the strong and the weak. Many evangelists travel around the world, spreading the message of Jesus Christ, but as seen in the Bible, not everyone felt worthy to speak on behalf of God. God chooses ordinary and common people to carry out His plan in reaching everyone and to accomplish his goals, see 1 Corinthians 1:26-28. In Psalm 28:7-8 and Isaiah 40:29-3, God gives strength to the weary, and He increases the power of the weak.

> *He said to them, "Go into all the world and preach the gospel to all creation.*
> *Mark 16:15*
> *New International Version (NIV)*

> *Therefore go and make disciples of all nations, baptizing them in the name of the Father and of the Son and of the Holy Spirit, and teaching them to obey everything I have commanded you. And surely I am with you always, to the very end of the age."*
> *Matthew 28:19-20*
> *New International Version (NIV)*

> *Declare his glory among the nations, his marvelous deeds among all peoples.*
> *Psalm 96:3*
> *New International Version (NIV)*

> *Brothers and sisters, think of what you were when you were called. Not many of you were wise by human standards; not many were influential; not many were of noble birth. But God chose the foolish things of the world*

to shame the wise; God chose the weak things of the world to shame the strong. God chose the lowly things of this world and the despised things—and the things that are not —to nullify the things that are, so that no one may boast before him.

1 Corinthians 1:26-28
New International Version (NIV)

The Lord is my strength and my shield; my heart trusts in him, and he helps me.

My heart leaps for joy, and with my song I praise him. The Lord is the strength of his people, a fortress of salvation for his anointed one.

Psalm 28:7-8
New International Version (NIV)

He gives strength to the weary and increases the power of the weak. Even youths grow tired and weary, and young men stumble and fall; but those who hope in the Lord will renew their strength. They will soar on wings like eagles; they will run and not grow weary, they will walk and not be faint.

Isaiah 40:29-31
New International Version (NIV)

Let's look at Moses. God chose him (Exodus 3:2-4 and Exodus 3:10) to lead the Israelites to the Promise Land. Since he did not see himself as eloquent in speech and not worthy of this calling, he asked God to use someone else; this is recorded in Exodus 4:10, Exodus 4:13, and Exodus 4:14-15. However, through many trials, he led the Israelites to the Promise Land with the help of God and his brother Aaron.

> *Moses saw that though the bush was on fire it did not burn up. So Moses thought, "I will go over and see this strange sight—why the bush does not burn up." When the Lord saw that he had gone over to look, God called to him from within the bush, "Moses! Moses!" And Moses said, "Here I am."*
> *Exodus 3:2-4*
> *New International Version (NIV)*

> *So now, go. I am sending you to Pharaoh to bring my people the Israelites out of Egypt."*
> *Exodus 3:10*
> *New International Version (NIV)*

> *Moses said to the Lord, "Pardon your servant, Lord. I have never been eloquent, neither in the past nor since you have spoken to your servant. I am slow of speech and tongue."*
> *Exodus 4:10*
> *New International Version (NIV)*

> But Moses said, "Pardon your servant, Lord. Please send someone else."
> *Exodus 4:13*
> *New International Version (NIV)*

> *Brothers and sisters, think of what you were when you were called. Not many of you were wise by human standards; not many were influential; not many were of noble birth. But God chose the foolish things of the world to shame the wise; God chose the weak things of the world to shame the strong. God chose the lowly things of this world and the despised things—and the things that are not —to nullify the things that are, so that no one may boast before him.*
>
> *Exodus 4:14-15*
> *New International Version (NIV)*

In the book of Acts, Peter and John were used by God by performing miracles, such as when Peter healed a lame beggar. These men were unschooled and common men, yet God chose these men to do extraordinary things. In 2Corinthians 11:6, Peter confirms that he is untrained as a speaker.

> *One day Peter and John were going up to the temple at the time of prayer—at three in the afternoon. Now a man who was lame from birth was being carried to the temple gate called Beautiful, where he was put every day to beg from those going into the temple courts. When he saw Peter and John about to enter, he asked them for money. Peter looked straight at him, as did John. Then Peter said, "Look*

at us!" So the man gave them his attention, expecting to get something from them.

Then Peter said, "Silver or gold I do not have, but what I do have I give you. In the name of Jesus Christ of Nazareth, walk." Taking him by the right hand, he helped him up, and instantly the man's feet and ankles became strong. He jumped to his feet and began to walk. Then he went with them into the temple courts, walking and jumping, and praising God.

Acts 3:1-8
New International Version (NIV)

When they saw the courage of Peter and John and realized that they were unschooled, ordinary men, they were astonished and they took note that these men had been with Jesus. But since they could see the man who had been healed standing there with them, there was nothing they could say.

Acts 4:13-14
New International Version (NIV)

I (Peter) may indeed be untrained as a speaker, but I do have knowledge. We have made this perfectly clear to you in every way.
2 Corinthians 11:6
New International Version (NIV)

- Peacemaker

Throughout Jesus' ministry, He demonstrated living in peace and without prejudice. His mission in part was to demonstrate how-to live-in peace even during a time of adversity.

The KJV Dictionary Defines peacemaker as follows:

> *PEACEMAKER, n. One who makes peace by reconciling parties that are at variance.*
> *Blessed are the peacemakers, for they shall be called the children of God. Matt.5.*[38]

Since the fall of Adam and Eve, sin has created a separation among people and between people and God. Adam and Eve's first two children were Cain and Abel. Cain was filled with jealousy, which resulted in Cain murdering Abel. Cain became jealous when God accepted Abel's offering first. The normal family rule was to accept the older brother's offering. This story is found in Genesis 4:4-5 and Genesis 4:8.

> *The Lord looked with favor on Abel and his offering, but on Cain and his offering he did not look with favor. So Cain was very angry, and his face was downcast.*
> *Genesis 4:4-5*
> *New International Version (NIV)*

---

[38] https://av1611.com/kjbp/kjv-dictionary/peacemaker.html

> *Now Cain said to his brother Abel, "Let's go out to the field." While they were in the field, Cain attacked his brother Abel and killed him.*
>
> *Genesis 4:8*
> *New International Version (NIV)*

We live in a world where violence, prejudice, racism, hate, and discrimination run rampant. As a Christian, it is our responsibility to be an example. When possible, we need to bring the conflict to an end and set aside whatever causes contention to live in peace with God and with one another. In so doing, one will fulfill the call to be peacemakers as recorded in Hebrews 12:14, Romans 12:19, and Matthew 5:9. As a peacemaker, when opportunities arise, we are to display the heart of Christ by surrendering our will. Even though we strive to be a peacemaker, we are to be aware that there are times when others are not willing to listen because their agenda is just to argue. Then it may be time to just step away from the issue and/or person.

> *Make every effort to live in peace with everyone and to be holy; without holiness no one will see the Lord.*
>
> *Hebrew 12:14*
> *New International Version (NIV)*

> *If it is possible, as far as it depends on you, live at peace with everyone.*
>
> *Romans 12:19*
> *New International Version (NIV)*

> *Blessed are the peacemakers, for they will be called children of God.*
>
> *Matthew 5:9*
> *New International Version (NIV)*

An example, taken from the Bible, was during a time when Jews and Samaritan's were not allowed to interact with each other. In John 4:1-9, Jesus was tired from His journey and sat near Jacob's Well, when a Samaritan woman approached the well to draw water. When Jesus asked for water from her, He broke the barriers not only for a class of people but also among races. Jesus made the two groups into one when he broke the wall of hostility; this is found in Ephesians 2:11-18. Just as Jesus broke the barriers between groups of people, we too must soften our hearts towards one another. This is possible when we surrender our will for the benefit of peace and relinquish the need to be proven right.

> *Now he had to go through Samaria. So he came to a town in Samaria called Sychar, near the plot of ground Jacob had given to his son Joseph. Jacob's well was there, and Jesus, tired as he was from the journey, sat down by the well. It was about noon. When a Samaritan woman came to draw water, Jesus said to her, "Will you give me a drink?" (His disciples had gone into the town to buy food.) The Samaritan woman said to him, "You are a Jew and I am a Samaritan woman. How*

can you ask me for a drink?" (For Jews do not associate with Samaritans.)

John 4:1-9
New International Version (NIV)

The Lord your God will circumcise your hearts and the hearts of your descendants, so that you may love him with all your heart and with all your soul, and live.

Deuteronomy 30:6
New International Version (NIV)

Therefore, remember that formerly you who are Gentiles by birth and called "uncircumcised" by those who call themselves "the circumcision" (which is done in the body by human hands) — remember that at that time you were separate from Christ, excluded from citizenship in Israel and foreigners to the covenants of the promise, without hope and without God in the world. But now in Christ Jesus you who once were far away have been brought near by the blood of Christ. For he himself is our peace, who has made the two groups one and has destroyed the barrier, the dividing wall of hostility, by setting aside in his flesh the law with its commands and regulations. His purpose was to create in himself one new humanity out of the two, thus making peace, and in one body to reconcile both of them to God through the cross, by which he put to death their hostility. He came and preached peace to you who were far away and peace to those who were near. For through him we both have access to the Father by one Spirit.

Ephesians 2:11-18
New International Version (NIV)

Circumcise your hearts, therefore, and do not be stiff-necked any longer. For the Lord your God is God of gods and Lord of lords, the great God, mighty and awesome, who shows no partiality and accepts no bribes.

Deuteronomy 10:16-17
New International Version (NIV)

For it is we who are the circumcision, we who serve God by his Spirit, who boast in Christ Jesus,

Philippians 3:3
New International Version (NIV)

 CHAPTER

9

Now Is the Time

Time is fleeting, and it seems we close our eyes and grow old overnight, and no one knows how much time they have before being called to meet God, their maker. Tomorrow is not promised, and therefore we need to respond to the call to come to God now before it is too late. Make the choice to accept Jesus, the only assurance we have of eternal salvation. In Romans 10:9-13, we are given details to accepting Jesus as Lord to be saved.

> *If you confess with your mouth that Jesus is Lord and believe in your heart that God raised him from the dead, you will be saved. For with the heart one believes and is justified, and with the mouth one confesses and is saved. For the Scripture says, "Everyone who believes in him will not be put to shame." For there is no distinction between Jew and Greek; for the same Lord is Lord of all, bestowing his riches*

> *on all who call on him. For "everyone who calls on the name of the Lord will be saved."*
> *Romans 10:9-13*
> *English Standard Version (ESV)*

Christianity is the only religion that guarantees salvation through the acceptance of Jesus, our Savior.

According to <u>Bible Talk</u> in the study, *"Bible Warfare, How to Defend Your Faith,"* several religions were compared. Here are a few of the religions that were recorded:

"Eastern Religions

Islam

The first is Islam from the Middle East, of course, Africa, and now all over the world. For Islam, salvation is accessed by practicing and repeating the five pillars. The five pillars of Islam are fasting, pilgrimage, giving alms, prayer, praying five times a day, and confessing that Muhammad is the Prophet. Continual practice of these things, the faithful practice of these things, is what saves you. An interesting thing about Islam, there's never really a hundred percent sure thing. If you talk to Muslims, they'll say, well, you can be saved, but if you're not, praise Allah anyways. So in Islam, you can do all the right things and still maybe not make it, because Allah thinks you're deficient in some way or another, that no one else is aware of but you, but he's aware of. In the Islamic religion, the only one hundred percent sure way to be in paradise is through death through jihad. That's the only one hundred percent sure way to be in paradise - that you die while fighting disbelievers. And the disbelievers are us, which may explain some of the allure.

You wonder, why are some young, perfectly healthy young men blowing themselves up. What's behind that? Well, in most of the country, unemployment is eighty percent. In Islam, you have to pay dowry; you need the money and other things to have a wife. And if you don't, you don't get a wife. So with very dim prospects of work, success, personal fulfillment, with very difficult prospects of having a wife or finding a wife if you're poor or don't have a lot of education, dying in a blaze of glory with the guarantee that you will be in paradise begins to look pretty good, especially if the leaders who are setting you up to blow yourself up pay your family a certain amount of money. Alright, so there's not just religious zeal behind suicide bombers; there's also the economic idea and the social pressure on many young men and young women. But basically, salvation is accessed through the practice of the five pillars.

Hinduism

Hinduism, the idea of salvation or the way to salvation is by eliminating evil in your life, until you are pure enough to merge with Brahma. In Hinduism, God does not have an individual personality; it is a force. You know in the Star Wars, in these movies, the force be with you. And people are saying, wow, what a concept. Where did they get that from? Well, they got it from Hinduism. That's where they got it from. The force be with you. That's the whole idea behind the Eastern religion, a great force. And of course, you continue to keep trying, life after life after life, to purify yourself before you finally pure - why do you think they're not and you're not allowed to kill a cow? People are starving in places, but you can't kill a cow, because many believe that the cow is the last reincarnation that you are transformed into before the next step of being taken up and merging with Brahma. So they don't want to spoil somebody's chance. Even to this day, I read an article a little while back that there was a big argument about this with the government. And the government came down on the side of their religious tradition and history. You still can't destroy these animals for food.

Christianity

Christianity is considered a Near Eastern religion because it started in Israel. Of course, it has spread all over the world. Basically, the idea of salvation in Christianity is that salvation is a gift from God based on faith in Jesus Christ. That's as compressed as I can make it. I know somebody will say, well, what about baptism? Well, sure. How do you express that faith? Well, you express it in repentance and baptism. But if you're going to just give a very brief succinct definition of salvation for Christianity, it's a gift from God accessed through faith in Jesus Christ."[39]

---

[39] https://bibletalk.tv/what-other-religions-teach-about-salvation

 CHAPTER

10

Conclusion

The call from God is to come to Him through Jesus Christ, our Savior, and Lord. Everyone needs to make this decision now before it is too late. As stated earlier, God does not want anyone to perish, but it is our responsibility to accept Jesus Christ. Eternity is a long time to suffer, tormented with fire and sulfur, and without any rest day and night, see Revelation 14:9-11and John 3:36. In Acts 4:12, 1Timothy 2:5, and Hebrews 7:24-25, we are reminded that there is no other way for eternal salvation. So, come just as you are as God is not looking for people that are perfect but broken and in need of a Savior. Revelations 22:17 tells us to come and receive the gift of eternal life.

> *"If anyone worships the beast and its image and receives its mark on their forehead or on their hand, they, too, will drink the wine of God's fury, which has been poured full strength into the cup of his wrath. They will be tormented with burning sulfur in the presence of the holy angels and of the Lamb. And the smoke of their torment will rise for*

ever and ever. There will be no rest day or night for those who worship the beast and its image, or for anyone who receives the mark of its name."

Revelation 14:9-11
New International Version (NIV)

Whoever believes in the Son has eternal life, but whoever rejects the Son will not see life, for God's wrath remains on them.

John 3:36
New International Version (NIV)

Salvation is found in no one else, for there is no other name under heaven given to mankind by which we must be saved."

Acts 4:12
New International Version (NIV)

For there is one God and one mediator between God and mankind, the man Christ Jesus.

1 Timothy 2:5
New International Version (NIV)

But because Jesus lives forever, he has a permanent priesthood. Therefore he is able to save completely those who come to God through him, because he always lives to intercede for them.

Hebrews 7:24-25
New International Version (NIV)

The Spirit and the bride say, "Come!" And let the one who hears say, "Come!" Let the one who is thirsty come; and let the one who wishes take the free gift of the water of life.

Revelation 22:17
New International Version (NIV)

Now is the time to accept Jesus Christ as your Savior, say yes before it is too late. Do not miss the call; time is shorter than you think.
Come!

About the Authur

The writer grew up with ten members in the family, seven siblings (eight children) in Los Angeles, California, where she was born. Her son Ben lives and works in Idaho.

She obtained a bachelor's degree from Cal State Fullerton in Business Accounting.

She worked for over 40 years in banks and a credit union. Her career began as a bank teller at the age of 17. As a Loan Officer, she approved and processed loans from small signature loans to corporate loans and anything in between. Her favorite type of loan was processing Real Estate Loans as she enjoyed the excitement as people purchased their residence. She retired as the Mortgage Servicing Administrator.

She is the writer of "Turn to God from Idols." This book explains what constitutes an idol and the benefits of staying away from them, and the consequence of worshiping idols.

Her love for God continues to grow as she studies and understands the magnitude of God's love for us, and she put her faith and trust in Him.

www.ingramcontent.com/pod-product-compliance
Lightning Source LLC
Chambersburg PA
CBHW071342080526